Nonprofit Organizations

Creating Membership through Communication

Trudy Milburn

California State University Channel Islands

HAMPTON PRESS, INC.
CRESSKILL, NJ 07626

Copyright © 2009 by Hampton Press, Inc.

All rights reserved. No part of this publication may be reproduced, stored in a retrieval system, or transmitted in any form or by any means, electronic, mechanical, photocopying, microfilming, recording, or otherwise, without permission of the publisher.

Printed in the United States of America

Library of Congress Cataloging-in-Publication Data

Milburn, Trudy.
  Nonprofit organizations : creating membership through communication / Trudy Milburn.
      p. cm. — (Social approaches to interaction series)
  Includes bibliographical references and index.
  ISBN 978-1-57273-882-9 (hbk.) — ISBN 978-1-57273-883-6 (pbk.)
1. Nonprofit organizations—Management. I. Title.
  HD2769.15.M55 2009
  658'.048—dc22
                                                    2009001224

Cover artwork © Sophie Blackall

Hampton Press, Inc.
23 Broadway
Cresskill, NJ 07626

Acknowledgments

I wish to thank Wendy Leeds-Hurwitz for having faith in this project and for offering excellent suggestions for improvement. My gratitude extends to Barbara and the folks at Hampton Press for adopting the project and working diligently to put it together. I also wish to thank the many colleagues who have discussed the data within these chapters informally and at conferences (in alphabetical order): Jana O'Keefe Bazzoni, Linda Blyer, Richard Buttny, Teresa Castor, Stephen Dandrow, Gary David, Larry Frey, Juan Gerena, Phillip Glenn, Alan Hansen, Heather Karjane, Jim Kenefick, Curtis LeBaron, Mark Mierswa, Laurie Ouellette, Gerry Philipsen, Anita Pomerantz, Gitte Rasmussen, Bob Sanders, Michelle Scollo, Stuart Sigman, Karen Tracy, Mike Vickery, Rick Wilkins, and Karen Wolf.

Thanks to Robert Myers and Baruch College for making "reassign time" possible to dedicate time to writing during the spring semester of 2006. In addition, two research awards from Baruch College, a Whiting Foundation Award and Drown Funds, contributed to my ability to complete this volume. I also appreciated the feedback from Baruch graduate students, who worked through this material in classes, and especially my research assistants Alethia Lambert and Komal Jadhwani.

Thanks to all of the members of the two nonprofit centers who shared with me their time and organization. Thanks to my friends Adam, Danielle, Cherie, and Nick for morning coffee conversations and to Sophie Blackall for providing the cover illustration. The Hatheways provided much needed moral support. Finally, I am particularly grateful to my parents, Chris and especially June, who offered their love and encouragement throughout this endeavor.

Contents

Preface	xi
Nonprofit Statistics	xii
Volunteering	xiii
Composition of Nonprofits	xiii
Why Nonprofits?	xiv
Nonprofits as Settings	xv
Introduction	1
Communication Perspective	2
Ethnography of Communication	2
Membership Categorization Analysis	4
Ethnomethodology	6
Combined Approaches	7
Culture in MCA, EC and Organizational Communication	9
Data Collection	10
Organizational Settings	12
Nuanced Membership	13
Chapter 1: Becoming a Participant/Becoming a Member	15
Membership Labels, Address and Reference	17
Distinguishing Members	17
Addressing Individual Members	19
Introductions	20
Initial Membership Categories	23
Chapter 2: Membership in a Community Context	25
PRC's Annual Dinner Dance	25
Community as Metaphor	26
Community Actions	27
Family Center Gala Anniversary Event	29
Location of Community	30
Community Struggles to Serve	30
Community History	32
Discussion	33

Contents

Chapter 3: Maintaining Membership through Meetings	37
Meeting Sequences and Norms	37
Meetings as Mundane	39
FC Decision Making	40
Valid Premises for Making Decisions	46
Outcomes of Decisions: Votes	50
Discussion	53
Summary	55
Chapter 4: Organizational Change	57
Strategic Change	58
Retreat	59
Long Term Planning	62
Terminating Membership/Ceasing to Participate	64
Terminating Membership	64
Situational Frame	67
What Change is Represented in this Account?	71
Summary	72
Chapter 5: Inscribing the Organization: Documents Structure Actions	73
The Use of Agendas	74
Minutes are Referenced	75
Secretaries Take Minutes	79
Questioning the Secretary's Role	81
Inscribing Conclusions	83
Chapter 6: Conclusions: Organization, Communication and Membership	85
Implications For Being a Member	85
Members Organize	88
Things Members Do	89
Members Communicate	90
Members Create Community	91
Members Create Nonprofits	91
Methodological Implications	91
Boarding "Pass"	93
Why Continue to Study Nonprofits?	94
Afterword	97
Notes	103
References	113
Author Index	123
Subject Index	127

Series Editor's Preface

This is the second book in the series Social Approaches to Interaction. Social approaches investigate communication as inherently collaborative, as joint constructions of meaning, and as embedded in a particular social or cultural context. This book fits this series because it applies several social approaches (ethnography of communication, membership categorization analysis, and ethnomethodology) to real contexts (nonprofit boards) and asks questions based on real people interacting (in this case, questions about identity, practice, and meaning). This book makes a substantial contribution to our understanding of organizational communication and identity management generally, and so it will be of interest to a wide array of readers.

Trudy Milburn has made several uncommon choices; together these demonstrate why this book merits publication and why it should find a wide audience. First, she has conducted long-term ethnographic research in not one but two contexts. Because ethnography requires a considerable time commitment, most such research only investigates a single context; examining two permits a greater understanding of what is unique about each, and what is more likely to be typical of similar contexts (in this case, other nonprofit boards). Second, her context is organizational communication, but specifically nonprofit organizations. Because most prior research has examined for-profit organizations, this volume fills a gap in our knowledge. Third, she has chosen to describe organizations where race and gender are at the forefront; a Puerto Rican center, and a family center, thus reminding us that not all organizational board members need be White and male. Fourth, she contributes to our understanding of membership as an interactional accomplishment, a topic appropriate for study in a wide variety of contexts beyond nonprofit boards. Fifth, she demonstrates how to appropriately combine theoretical approaches that are often viewed as quite distinct, if not contradictory; ethnography of communication, membership categorization, and ethnomethodology. Many Language and Social Interaction scholars within the discipline of Communication have stopped paying attention to ethnomethodology, given that ethnography and conversation analysis are more frequent approaches; Milburn reminds us of what ethnomethodology can contribute to our understanding of interaction. Sixth, she provides an appendix with specific recommendations for practitioners who might serve on nonprofit boards in the future, thus speaking to an audience beyond the academy. Academic research is not an end in and of itself; at least the implications of academic research should always be made accessible to interested practitioners.

—Wendy Leeds-Hurwitz

Preface

There is a growing public awareness of the existence of special services provided by nonprofit organizations. Along with this awareness, much confusion exists about which organizations are indeed nonprofit. What comes to mind for most people is the large variety of organizations that are subsumed under the nonprofit label. These include: "churches, hospitals, soccer camps and Little League baseball, schools and universities, think tanks and research institutes, theaters and symphony orchestras, civil rights and environmental groups" (O'Neill, 2002, p. xvii).

Most often nonprofits are defined by what they are not. Some have posited that any group that is not a family, not a businesses, or not part of government counts as a nonprofit organization. The standard definitions include several common features, such as being "institutional" (O'Neill, 2002) or having some kind of "organizational structure" (Salamon, Anheier, List, Toepler, Sokolowski, and Associates, 1999); being "private" (O'Neill, 2002) or not from the state (Salamon et al., 1999); being "self-governing" (O'Neill, 2002; Salamon et al., 1999), yet have blurred lines of ownership and accountability (Frumkin, 2002); and usually operating for the public's benefit (O'Neill, 2002, p. 2).

The term *nonprofit* has been called a misnomer because "it is perfectly legal for a nonprofit to make a profit" (Berry, 2003, p. 5). However, the distinction is that nonprofit organizations do not *distribute* profits (Frumkin, 2002; O'Neill, 2002; Salamon et al., 1999). The people who benefit from a nonprofit are those who are "served," rather than "owners" of the organization. Nonprofit organizations do not have owners.

A final feature of nonprofits is the distinct relationship employees have with the organization. Although nonprofit organizations do employ a staff, they are often described as involving noncoercive participation (Frumkin, 2002). Many of those who work with nonprofits organizations are volunteers because there are few staff members who are paid. This volunteer aspect distinguishes nonprofits most from "for-profit" organizations. It is this "noncompulsory" aspect of work that is often described by volunteers as meaningful participation (O'Neill, 2002). In order to operate, nonprofits rely on voluntary membership and/or contributions (see Salamon et al., 1999, p. 3).

Nonprofit Statistics

Within the United States, nonprofits operate as one of the four sectors that include the household sector, the government sector, the for-profit or business sector, and the not-for-profit or nonprofit sector (O'Neill, 2002). On the global level, nonprofits are described as fitting into the "civil society" sector. This sector includes private community groups, health clinics, schools, day-care centers, environmental organizations, cultural institutions, professional associations, and consumer groups. Whether national or international nonprofits, the size of these sectors is large and growing. As of 2000, "the U.S. nonprofit sector consisted of 1.5 million nonprofit organizations registered with the IRS, an additional 300,000 religious organizations, and an unknown number of unregistered groups" (O'Neill, 2002, p. 9). According to another source (NCCSdataweb.urban.org), the number of nonprofit organizations grew 28.8% from 1996 to 2004 (from 1,084,897 to 1,397,263 organizations). The nonprofit sector accounts for between 5 to 10% of the U.S. economy. It employs more civilian employees than the federal government and the 50 state governments combined; making up about 8% of the nation's noninstitutional civilian employees. The nonprofit sector employs more people than any of the following industries: agriculture; mining; construction; transportation, communication, and other public utilities; finance; insurance; and real estate (O'Neill, 2002).

The nonprofit sector is thought to be much larger than statistics are able to illuminate because smaller groups such as "book clubs, support groups, choirs, bridge clubs, Bible-study groups, hobby clubs, garden societies, investment groups, neighborhood improvement associations, softball teams, volunteer bands, and orchestras" (O'Neill, 2002, p. 13) and others do not file with the IRS as 501(c)(3) organizations.

Globally, the civil sector generates revenue that exceeds the gross domestic product (GDP) of all but six foreign countries: Japan, Germany, the United Kingdom, France, Italy, and China. Overall, this sector represents $1.1 trillion. Nonprofits amount to the world's eighth-largest economy that employs more people than the largest private firms. According to Salamon et al. (1999), two thirds of nonprofits serve three traditional welfare areas: education (30% of total); health (20%); and social services (18%). Fifty-five percent of volunteer time goes into two principal fields: recreation (including sports) and social services. The focus on these areas varies by region. For instance, Salamon et al. (1999) suggests four patterns: most of Western Europe is focused on welfare services, including education and health or social service organizations; Central Europe focuses on recreation and culture; Latin America focuses on education; and other developed countries (including the United States, Japan, Australia and Israel) are primarily composed of health care and education nonprofits.

By revenue, there are a hierarchy of types, with hospitals and health care having the largest share (O'Neill, 2002), followed by social assistance, and social advocacy, performing arts, museums, historical sites, and civic and social organizations. Educational services make up the smallest share.

Although some erroneously equate governments with more social services as having fewer nonprofit organizations, this has been found to be largely untrue. Data on 22 countries studied gave "no support" to this theory (Salamon et al., 1999). For instance, among the 11 countries with relatively high levels of government social welfare spending, five had smaller nonprofit sectors and six had relatively large ones. Among the 11 countries with relatively low levels of welfare protections, eight had smaller nonprofit sectors and three had relatively large nonprofit sectors (Salamon et al., 1999). Contrary to some popular beliefs, the United States does *not* "have the world's largest nonprofit sector after all, at least when measured as a share of total employment" (Salamon et al., 1999, p. 12).

Volunteering

One prominent feature of nonprofits is the number of volunteers employed by them. According to O'Neill (2002), although they themselves are not paid, volunteers donate the most money to the organizations for which they work. "People who volunteer, as well as those who attend religious services more frequently, are more likely than others to give and to give more generously" (O'Neill, 2002, p. 28). The relationships formed by attendance and involvement often influence where one makes a monetary contribution.

In addition, members of the board of directors often give large sums to the nonprofit because they believe in its cause (Drucker, 1989). Directors have often been volunteers before they served on the boards (Drucker, 1989); this demonstrates deep commitment and knowledge of the organization.

"In 1998 an estimated 109 million American volunteered, contributing 20 billion hours through organizations and on a person-to-person basis" (O'Neill, 2002, p. 30). This size of the volunteer labor force that is used in nonprofit organizations goes largely unrecognized, but is essential for the operation of the work that is performed by these organizations.

Composition of Nonprofits

In a 1992 diversity study, nonprofit boards were dominated by members who were classified as White or caucasian (Duca, 1996). Women made up on average only 8.5 seats of boards with 21 members. Seventy-one percent of the survey respondents reported that it was "important" to have a culturally diverse board of directors, but only 36.5% had a "diversity policy" in place. One theory is that boards believed they did not need diversity because the people they served were not diverse, nor did their mission or goals require diversity. According to the authors of this survey, 79% of those surveyed indicated a lack of awareness of the importance of diversity among staff and board members (Duca, 1996).

Why Nonprofits?

Associations have been described as "interstitial" or "mediation" institutions (O'Neill, 2002) that protect the smaller, weaker elements of society while also making the larger, powerful elements more responsive. Their status as the underdog of organizations, as serving rather than selling, as places where people come to work voluntarily (often after their paid job), and as local places situated in neighborhoods where people live, all give the nonprofits an unusual status among organizations. Further, they are unusual because volunteers often work with the people who are served by the organization face-to-face. All of those who participate are people who live near one another, who have common goals, or who may be similar in many ways.[1]

Nonprofit organizations' status as "in-between" organizations makes their boundaries unclear. The traditional lines between donors, clients, board members, workers, and local communities can blur as one participant can play many of these roles at one time or another.

Nonprofit organizations can address problems that the market (or government) does not address. Usually, a nonprofit organization is created because its founders see a problem or a need in a community (see also Drucker, 1989). This is a profoundly different starting point than a for-profit organization, which begins with a product or service to sell (and often create a need afterward). Nonprofit organizations can be more creative in solving problems for those (customers) who do not pay. Nonprofits demand creativity and unique ways of creating services to make them available to those in need, as well as in identifying who is in need.

Although a "customer focus" has been in vogue for several years within the business world, this perspective has been called a focus on the "demand side" rather than a "supply side" focus that examines the "givers" of time or money (Frumkin, 2002). This difference in perspective is important to acknowledge. If one examines how tasks are accomplished and how workers *express* their values and commitment by choosing specific organizations to which they will volunteer and donate, then one can learn what communities consider important (Frumkin, 2002).

Another reason to focus on nonprofits is the different relationships that exist between members of nonprofits and for-profit organizations. Boden (1994), for instance, has characterized the relationships between employees and customers to organizations as mere "pawns." This relationship is based on the power commanded by organizations. "From government bureaucracies and faceless firms such as oil companies and financial conglomerates to the quite local tyranny of traffic conditions and slow-moving queues at the supermarket, organizational society dominates every horizon" (Boden, 1994, p. 108; see also Bakan, 2004). Although it is true that nonprofits are organizations, participants have a very different relationship with these organizations.

One significant type of relationship is participating as a member of the board of directors. Houle (1989) argues that despite the distinctions between different organizations, "all boards share a common form and have basic similarities in how they operate" (p. 2). He describes this as is a tripartite structure to get work done, dividing participants into board, staff, and executive.[2] A board is "an organized group of people with the authority collectively to control and foster an institution that is usually administered by a qualified executive and staff" (Houle, 1989, p. 6). This ability to control the work of others suggests that board members and their behavior should be examined closely if one wants to learn about how nonprofit organizations work.

Nonprofits as Settings

Setting an ethnographic study in nonprofit organizations necessarily highlights the features of these kinds of organizations as socially distinct entities. Because nonprofits exist and are based on governmental definitions, these definitions and statistics are important to consider. However, due to the prominence of nonprofit organizations, in the United States and abroad, this social category warrants further consideration. Although these organizations certainly warrant closer examination, their constitution as organizations was not the starting point of my study.

Originally, I wanted to examine ethnic identity. I believe that this can be best achieved by examining how it is enacted interactionally. One place to examine the doing of it is obviously a center devoted to promoting a particular culture. Accordingly, I began to volunteer at the Puerto Rican Center. When, at the conclusion of this study, I was asked how my data demonstrated ethnic identity and not just the identity of the organization, I sought another center for comparison. This comparison created the sample of two nonprofit organizations that form the data for my claims about nonprofit organizations.

Members themselves orient to their organization as a nonprofit. Consider the following statement made by one board member during a board meeting about the idea of getting someone as a financial advisor:

> Jeffrey: That's the thing, I think you can, *nonprofits* deal with this stuff all the time and I know that one of the boards when I was in law school actually, had, you know, financial advisors volunteer their services and I just assumed that in [this city], you probably, I mean, I could try to kind of, ask around (italics added).

When an organization is a nonprofit, members know it. They also act in ways that define it as a nonprofit. That is, the definition is not only a governmental tax status definition. Members create the nonprofit organization based on what they know about nonprofits, and what they figure out in the doing of being in a nonprofit. Even though all of the board members were volunteers, and one knows that some places—such as law firms—and some people—such as lawyers or accountants—*do* volunteer their time to assist nonprofit organizations, this Family Center never did (during my tenure) have someone volunteer in this capacity.

Therefore, the sheer numbers of nonprofit organizations, the size of the sector, the kinds or areas that are served by the sector, such as health care and education, are only a small part of what it means to be a nonprofit organization. Those facts or statistics give a small part of the story. The story of the mundane work within a nonprofit and how the members themselves create a sense of what it means to volunteer their time to create the organization is the story that this book was written to tell.

Introduction

> *Membership categories are not to be presumed* a priori; *they are a matter for empirical investigation*
>
> —Hester and Elgin (1997, p. 3)

Who are the board members of nonprofit organizations today? We do not know much about these members unless we happen to have the opportunity to join such a board. I have had such opportunities and have found that the distinctions between board member, mother, secretary, or Puerto Rican (often perceived as distinct identity features) are more blurred than reported in research studies. Frequently, one category, such as the gender or ethnicity of board members, is taken as the most prominent feature. However, membership in any such category, being a woman and a board member, or being Puerto Rican and a board member, is relevant only in some conversations. How the boundaries of any specific membership category become prominently featured in interaction is a key question in determining the boundaries of the organization itself.

Shortly after questioning who is part of an organization, one often questions how the organization itself shapes its employees. Organizational identity has been the topic of several articles (see Albert & Whetten, 1985; Elsbach & Kramer, 1996; Hogg & Terry, 2000; Hogg, Terry, & White, 1995; Scott & Lane, 2000). This literature often poses a unified public perception of an identity that organizational participants either share or not. Organizational identity is considered a feature of the organization that is management-created and enforced. Identity in these articles often refers to public perception, or individual conformity to a managerial ideal. Rarely is social identity, or the way participants create a sense of a collective identity, the main focus (for an exception, see Cheney, 1991). In this volume, I focus on the way organizations themselves are created and maintained through the coordinated actions of the people who comprise them. A major premise of this work is that *member* discourse, rather than what is often referred to as organizational identity, creates and constitutes the organization and work itself.[3]

Communication Perspective

In order to learn about member discourse, I take a communication perspective, which differs from a managerial perspective. Rather than understanding "the work" as something that managers delineate and delegate, the work is understood as something that is socially negotiated, defined in the moment of interaction by supervisors and subordinates (see Boden, 1994). The traditional hierarchal perspective of organizations suggests that communication functions merely as a channel through which tasks are passed down through the ranks, from the board of directors down through managers, to the front-line staff. A communication-centric perspective does not deny that hierarchy may influence the way conversations and work are conducted, but shifts the focus from the structure of the organization to those who are engaged in the activities of the organization—to any member who speaks in order to get work done.

Viewed from a communication perspective, the individual employee does not warrant specific investigation. What is important is not how an individual feels about an organization nor about his or her subjective experience as an organizational member; rather, it is the relationships that individuals (employees or board members) create with one another in the process of communicating that comprise a "member discourse."

Member discourse can be examined through a variety of lenses. However, there are three research traditions that are best equipped to examine such discourse. These are the ethnography of communication (Carbaugh, 1989; Hymes, 1972, 1974; Philipsen, 1975, 1976, 1986), membership categorization analysis (Hester & Elgin, 1997; Sacks, 1995), and ethnomethodology (Garfinkel, 1967). These three traditions are not only research analytic tools, but can be understood as theoretical perspectives from which to understand how organizations and, more particularly, how the *people* in those organizations, get things done by doing what they do.[4]

In this introductory chapter, each tradition is described and examined in relation to the other. The remaining chapters highlight specific instances of interaction and interactional moments within the life of particular organizations in order to understand how conversational participants identify members and determine not only who counts as a valued member (see also Wieder & Pratt, 1990), but how organizations are socially structured by members.

Ethnography of Communication

Ethnography of communication attracts scholars who are interested in participating in the lives of a particular community. The project holds the assumption that a speech community is composed of members who share ways of communicating that are distinct from other groups. In the process of conducting research, participating in the activities of the group, and speaking with various group members, communication patterns become evident. Key terms for speaking, acting, and knowing are noted by the researcher, as are particular ways of conducting social life. Following time spent in the field, the researcher composes a story about the people with whom she lived in order to help others learn about such practices and, ultimately, refine our theories of communication.

Since the research of Hymes, who was most keen on learning about distinct ways of speaking, several questions have driven such studies. These include questions of identity ("Who are these people?"); practice ("How do these people do what they do?"); and meaning ("How do these people make sense of what they do?").[5] Researchers committed to ethnography of communication hold the perspective that social life is constructed through the process of communication and that studying communication practices will hold the keys to discovering more about a community's culture (including values and beliefs).

Throughout the project, there have been two different approaches to research. Dell Hymes (1962, 1972) advocated starting with a "speech community." Philipsen (1975), for instance, began his research with a group in a particular geographic location. Once there, he was able to find out who speaks to whom, in what places, and with what meanings. A second approach is to begin with communicative practices. For instance, Carbaugh (1989) found patterned ways of speaking and then, because they were made by people with various affiliations (men, women, young, old, religious, nonreligious, Black, White, etc.) within the same geographic area—the United Stated—he labeled those practices, "American."

Often researchers from this tradition privilege one or more components of the analytic mnemonic, S.P.E.A.K.I.N.G. that Hymes (1972) set forth in order to systematize the collection of data among groups with distinctive speaking practices. These features include the Setting or scene within which people speak, the Participants themselves, the Ends or goals of speech, the speech Acts, the Key or tone, the Instrumentalities or channels, and the Norms and Genres. Those researchers who are concerned with the Participants examine closely the people in the speech community and how their interaction indicates social roles they occupy. Carbaugh (1994) suggested the use of the term *personhood* to describe the sense of identity of the participants. However, although this term was introduced to try to move away from the identity of any one participant, it still connotes the sense of an individual. This term has not been used consistently, and other researchers continue to refer to the way that participants interact as creating individual and social identities as well as "social relationships."

When Hymes (1962) began his research program on ethnography of speaking, he was concerned about maintaining precision when describing the communication practices of particular groups, both in terms of their boundaries and their own labels, taking seriously how members use language and other communicative practices[6] to help construct a sense of communal membership; and to attend to how the overlapping boundaries of people in the various communities can be distinguished. Some of these commitments have been taken up by scholars who have drawn on an ethnography of communication (EC) perspective to study organizations (Bailey, 1997; Carbagh, 1988; Covarrbias, 2002; Rudd, 1995, 2000; Schwartzman, Kneifel, & Krause, 1978; Sequeira, 1993). Considering that, since its inception, the program of ethnography of communication has been based on finding a group that could be defined as a "speech community," the studies that have used an organization as a speech community are few.

Membership Categorization Analysis

Within the field of communication, Harvey Sacks' work has been known as the root of conversation analysis (Atkinson & Heritage, 1984; Glenn, LeBaron, & Mandelbaum, 2003; Holtgraves, 2002). However, in other disciplines such as sociology, Sacks' work is understood as branching off in two distinct directions (CA and MCA): one that focuses on the sequential organization of talk and the other that looks more closely at categories (Hester & Elgin, 1997; Housley & Fitzgerald, 2002; Lepper, 2000; Stokoe, 2004). Within communication, until recently the only reference to membership categorization analysis has been in the area of gender studies (see Hanson, 2005[7]; Hopper & LeBaron, 1998; Pomerantz & Mandelbaum, 2005; Stokoe & Smithson, 2001).

In general, researchers who use membership categorization analysis have taken as their starting point a segment of conversation and looked for signs that reveal information about the groups to which speakers belong. Although initially some of these conversations were recorded from a group therapy session (Sacks, 1995), the groups with which conversational participants identified ("hotrodders") was explicitly *not* the group in therapy. So, rather than starting with a group to find out how members' identify, this technique presupposes that information about members' group affiliations may be present in any conversation.

In order to learn more about how people speak about their group identities, Sacks (1995) looked for an "apparatus" that was used by the speakers. He discovered what he came to call a "membership categorization device" that he defined as

> any collection of membership categories, containing at least a category, which may be applied to some population containing at least a member, so as to provide, by the use of some rules of application, for the pairing of at least a population member of a categorization device members. A device is then a collection plus rules of application. (Sacks, 1995, p. 246)

Hester and Elgin (1997) have refined the conceptual framework for membership categorization analysis. Because Sacks' definition did not specify that a "member" is a person,[8] Hester and Elgin (1997) reformulated the definition of member categories as "classifications or social types that may be used to describe persons" (p. 3). These categories are applied by using a variety of rules that Sacks posited. Hester and Elgin (1997) describe the first as the "economy rule," which suggests that a preference will be made for placing persons in one single category. Sacks' emphasis was slightly different; he stated,

> It may be observed that if a member uses a single category from any membership categorization device then they can be recognized to be doing *adequate reference* to a person. (Sacks, 1995, p. 246)

By emphasizing "adequate reference" as the point of the rule, Sacks is not necessarily suggesting that a member be placed in only one category; rather, that, when making reference to a person, one need only use a single category. For instance, Sacks (1989) notes that one can ask, "which, for some set, are you?" (p. 271). However, in his lecture on the M.I.R.[9] device, Sacks (1989) affirms that he is *not* talking about groups in the traditional sociological sense of "groups, organized groups, organizations" (p. 272). In order to come to the idea of groups, he posited a second rule.

The second rule has come to be known as the "consistency rule." Sacks (1995) stated,

> If some population of persons is being categorized and if a category for some device's collection has been used to categorize a first member of the population, then that category or other categories of the same collection *may* be used to categorize further members of the population. (p. 246)

This rule helps us move from categorizing a single member in a single category to a collection of members in a population of like persons (not necessarily geographic). These two rules form the "machinery" that participants use in their conversations to connote membership. Further, because the conversations illustrate membership, what Sacks calls "mutual elaboration"[10] is the key to understanding the impact of "communication" on membership. Each conversational participant works to elaborate parts of each member category.

Because conversations are used to find this machinery, some may wonder how MCA differs from the methodology of conversation analysis (CA). Hester and Elgin (1997) explain that CA is concerned with sequential analysis, whereas MCA is concerned with categorizational aspects of social interaction. However, they also state that these two methods can inform one another. For instance, social identity provides for a sense of the (sequentially organized) talk, just as the talk provides for a sense of social identity. Teachers, for example, establish their credentials as incumbents of such a category through the production of particular sorts of sequentially positioned utterances, just as their utterances trade-off a presumed social identity (as teachers) for their accountable production and recognition. (pp. 2–3)

Penelope Eckert (1989) provides a superb example of a membership categorization analysis by undertaking participant observation in a high school. By examining student conversations, Eckert focuses on the ways that the students create categories that they use to organize themselves and create meaning for their actions. As students, they are not institutional members who are in positions of power to make the rules and, therefore, they categorize persons (and populations) into groups of "jocks" and "burn-outs" with their own rules and meanings.

Although MCA studies have been conducted based on a variety of interactions (police, news, family caregiving, ethnicity, mental health, travel agency calls, talk radio, and schools), the analyses usually lead to a discussion about the way members *organize* as one of the most salient features of what members do. Therefore, although not specifically confined to a selection of organizations, MCA provides the tools that can help us to learn more about any particular organization (see also Psathas, 1999).[11]

Ethnomethodology

Another tradition proposed by Garfinkel (1967) examines the way members organize themselves. He called this ethnomethodology (EM). This research tradition focuses specifically on the ways members devise and use their own "methods" for getting things done.

Although the general theoretical stance suggests that we learn more about how members make up rules for their actions, the most famous way that Garfinkel began examining these patterns were his "breech studies." Initially, though, he did differentiate his "documentary" method from other methods by describing how "membershipping" demonstrated how patterns emerged and were managed by members (Garfinkel, 1967, p. 94). Often, other methods, such as EC or MCA, have served as analytic tools to uncover members' practices.

It has been claimed that ethnomethodological studies of work started with "Harvey Sacks' observation that the local production of social order existed as an orderliness of conversational practice" (Garfinkel, 1986, p. vii). Since then, ethnomethodological research has been extended by David Sudnow's "ethnographic materials" of jazz ensembles. The "detailed observations" provided by ethnography afford the researcher "insights as to what situations would be about" (Girton, 1986, p. 69).

Introduction 7

The collaboration between Garfinkel and Sacks (1986) further explicates how to examine members' methods. They suggest looking for four different types of methods that can be examined: "sets of alternatives;" "factual character[istics] of information;" "circumstances of choice;" and "rationale [for the] properties of individual and concerted actions" (p. 163).

Combined Approaches

There are many similarities between the ethnography of communication, membership categorization analysis, and ethnomethodology. The two most salient features include an attention to the boundaries of the "group" ("Who is included?"), and the specifics of the practice ("What is said distinctly?"). These common commitments, although phrased differently, both speak to the primacy of communicating "relationships" between interactants.

For EC, one either begins with a pattern of speech and then uses that pattern to locate the boundaries of its community of users, or one finds a geographic area where distinct speaking patterns can be heard and then upon listening, learns the boundaries of such a community. MCA attends to the member label first and then determines, by closely examining conversations, how that member label is attached or attributed to particular groups of people. Ethnomethodologist begin by participating with or as members[12] and then figure out how members organize themselves.[13] Combining EM, MCA and EC one can posit the following three steps for conducting research:

1. Find a label for persons
2. Recognize that these persons engage in normative practices
3. Posit a "Membership Category"

Simply, once a label is heard, it indicates both a person as well as a practice. Both traditions focus on key terms that are used by group members and "normative practices" that are enacted by those who count as members. Patterned practices are often determined to be based on social norms (N in the S.P.E.A.K.I.N.G. mnemonic). Further, Sacks (1995) includes norms in his description of what it means to be a member. For instance, he describes how practices that mothers engage in refer to their membership category, label, and norms.

> [That] mommies ought to soothe their crying babies ... is not simply ... a maxim for good behavior for mommies, but that one can use it to see who it is that's doing something which it can characterize. (p. 253)

By noting normative behaviors for one category (mommies), one recognizes the implication of others in that "category set" (babies). Membership, then, is not simply a label that is used ("mommy" or "baby"), but how that label is used to refer to proper actions that are taken with regard to others in the category set ("The baby *cried*. The mommy *picked it up.*").

Likewise, the idea of "membership" has been invoked in EC. Philipsen (1989) describes the two parts of what he calls "membering" as including both the speaker acting as a member, as well as recognizing that his own speech is like the group with which he identifies. Further, he asserts, "to know, and to use appropriately, the meanings, rules, and speech habits of a local group signals and affirms that one is a member of it" (Philipsen, 1992, p. 14). In sum, "speech is both an act of and a resource for 'membering'" (Philipsen, 1992, p. 14).

Weider (1999) describes the intersections between ethnomethodoology (EM), conversation analysis, and ethnography of speaking.[14] He suggests the overlap consists in their relationship with research that posits phemomenon as "over there" versus studying by engaging interaction; keen attention to setting; the importance of members' attention to what is important in their own conversations; the importance of context and presence to how issues are interactionally worked out *in situ*; direct observation; and the development of norms where what people "should do" is worked out (p. 167). He claims these methods are "sufficiently synchronized" (p. 168) in each methodology that a researcher observes similar phenomena, just in different terms.

The richness of a combination of what some see as distinct strands of research can add a texture for understanding membership that cannot be accomplished by the use of either method alone. By starting with EM and EC, in spending time listening to, and participating with, a group of people and then analyzing the data through an MCA lens and focusing on how members create categories, one begins to figure out who the people are and how they matter to one another and what is it that they are creating together.

In sum, analyzing membership includes learning about:

- How members use terms (indexicals) that are familiar to other members.
- Recognizing that members do not say everything (they leave out words) because other members infer the rest.
- How members are recognizable to other members, by virtue of some shared features (verbal or nonverbal).
- How members are accountable to one another for their actions—and are prepared to give accounts of their actions that are sensible from members' perspectives—based on a set of shared standards/norms.

The conclusions that are arrived at often lead to descriptions of members' cultures.

Culture in MCA, EC and Organizational Communication

Although EC and MCA studies were published together in one volume during their formative years[15] (see Gumperz & Hymes, 1972), they have since followed divergent paths. When considering bringing them back together, what counts as "culture" seems to be both a point of contestation as well as a point of agreement (see also Sidnell, 2006). For instance, Hester and Elgin (1997) question whether culture is a pregiven set of rules and knowledge by which members know how to act together, or something that is learned, defined, and redefined through interaction, as members together co-determine rules and member categories in and through their talk. This criticism may stem from ethnographic reports that have tended to create a story about a particular culture without adequately demonstrating *how* participants communicated in actual moments of interaction, suggesting that the researcher relied too heavily on field notes rather than attending to more detailed interactional moments.

Similarly, within the organizational communication literature, culture has moved from a prominent place to one that has come under increasing scrutiny. Since the writing of Deal and Kennedy (1982) and Pacanowsky and O'Donnell Trujillo (1983), cultural stories, jargon, and rituals have been examined to learn about the common beliefs and values of organizational participants. These studies of shared meaning systems have moved from what an organization *has* to what it *is* (Smircich & Calas, 1987). Although culture was considered a "guiding metaphor," it has also had its share of critiques that suggest that the concept of culture has not met its ideals. For instance, Meyerson and Martin (as cited in Frost, Moore, Reis Louis, Lundberg, & Martin, 1991) take issue with a holistic and unitary view of culture. They suggest that organizational cultures are more aptly described in different phases of coming together as a united whole (integration) to coming apart (fragmentation). Knuf (1993) likewise condemns, "Contrary to its suggestive designation, organization culture theory is not emic, ethnomethodological: Unfortunately, it deals only rarely with the concepts of interpretations generated by organizational members in and for their everyday lives" (pp. 62–63). Similarly, Schein (1991) notes that the commitment to observe the behavior of cultural members is rarely borne out in ethnographic reports that he finds "conceptually vague," and only focus on a small set of observable phenomenon rather than generalizing to broader implications (p. 245).

I share the concern that through ethnography of communication, a researcher can readily assume that, by examining a speech community, one gains adequate information[16] to make claims about a larger category, a culture (see also Baumann, 1996). It is often the case that the reports about specific speech communities progress automatically to claims about culture simply because its "members" share a "way of speaking." Further, claims that particular ways of speaking imply beliefs about being and acting are stated without hesitation. However, the critiques do not necessary rely on ethnography of communication scholars' own descriptions about the cultural claims they are making.

Philipsen (1987) describes three ways of defining culture—as code, as conversation, and as community. The first refers to the stable system of beliefs and values, the second refers to the patterned interaction, the third, "draws attention to a human grouping whose members claim commonality derived from shared identity" (p. 249). He advocates for a use of all three to form a "comprehensive insight" into culture. Carbaugh (2005) postulates what he calls a "focal dimension" of cultural conversations, "the presumption and expression of shared identity, that is the expressive orientation of interactants to a common social and cultural life" (p. 157). Both of these definitions provide what Schein (1991) suggests are the benefits of using ethnographic methods for examining concept of culture. He claims that it helps us to understand (a) stability over time, (b) similarity or sharing between members, (c) patterned behavior, (d) the historical process of culture as it is enacted, and (e) influences on all areas of life.

In agreement with Hester and Elgin's (1997) description of MCA as "culture in action," I believe that we can prevent hasty conclusions about practices equaling culture. Sacks (1995) has suggested that culture is a name for an apparatus that tells us "how it is that any activities which members do in such a way as to be recognizable as such to members, are done, and done recognizably" (p. 245). Both Eckert (1989) and Moerman[17] (1974) provide studies that serve as exemplars for analyzing interactions for member labels of persons and behaviors (including ways of speaking) from a combined ethnographic/MCA analysis to posit shared values and beliefs. The focus is on the communal activities of *doing* culture as relational participants, rather than the static, being of it.

Data Collection

The examples in this book stem from a collection of data over a lengthy span of time. Although membership can be described as evident in any one conversation (see Sacks' examples), the gathering of organizational conversations over time (12 months in the first; 2 years in the second) is a key component in any claim about the sustaining value of any particular membership form of talk. Because communication is a process that requires participants to consider the past and future when making interpretations of utterances or symbolic action, examining it over time is one of the only ways to capture a broader understanding of the indexicals and what has been left unsaid. Thus, the steps that were taken include the following:

1. Participant Observation: a data collection method
2. Recordings: audio and video—data collection method
3. Field Notes: data collection and analysis methods
4. Analysis: data analysis methods

The first demonstrates a commitment to the process of learning how things are done by having to do them. The second step is required in order to capture the ongoing flow of conversation as it occurs. The third is often used to supplement the second, as one observes, one takes notes of particular communicative actions that are noticeable in the scene. Often researchers report that these notes are taken retrospectively, at some time after the interaction was observed (see Clifford & Marcus, 1986). However, I was afforded the unique opportunity of taking notes during meetings as the recording secretary—creating a space in the margin for my notes while faithfully noting down what was said during each meeting. Finally, the audio- and videorecordings were listened to (or watched) repeatedly, selections were transcribed, and then selections underwent a multipronged analysis for finding member categories as distinct terms and how the conversational sequence made meaningful particular sayings. In addition to these basic steps, I collected various organizational documents—such as mailings, schedules, announcements, memos, and e-mails (from the second site)—in order to find out how such member categories were inscribed by members themselves (not only through my notes).

Members used several ways to indicate meaning. The first are membership labels, which can be found by examining individual or group address, reference terms, or pronoun usage. Although these are common categories by which membership is designated, what such terms mean to members can most fruitfully be understood in the context in which they occur. The definition of "context" is and has been contested,[18] however, the context of usage is the one I believe stays closest how members make relevant particular topics by their word choice. One can use the sequence in which any member terms are used in order to determine how or what members mean by the terms. Meaning, therefore, includes (a) what to label whom, when, and for what purposes; (b) when such labeling or referring occurs, what kinds of activities or accounts happen next to reify or reject such terms?; (c) when the labeling refers to individuals or larger groups, is such a label adopted by subsequent speakers unproblematicly, or rejected and a new term used in its place? These three issues help to demonstrate that members' language use and frequency, not just singly as individuals, but in coordinating their actions with others, is the way membership is constituted.

Organizational Settings

The focus of the present text is the way that nonprofit organizations are member-defined. The organizations have legal rules that define their boundaries as organizations. The two organizations that will serve as data are defined as IRS designated, nonprofit, 501(c) (3) organizations (http://www.irs.gov/charities/nonprofits/index.html). Both are community centers whose members pay dues. Dues and other fundraisers provide the primary income stream. They are overseen by a board of directors who are elected from and by the membership. Again, although "membership" is part of the form and structure of the organization, it is also something that happens in and through the conversations made by those who participate in any organizational activity.

Therefore, the boundedness of the organizations in question is

1. a legal definition;
2. comprised of statements that label the group as an organization.

The labels used to refer to the two organizations supplied, as examples in this text are, the Puerto Rican Center and the Family Center.[19] Both are located in the Northeast in two different major metropolitan cities. Two organizations were examined in order to compare what was distinct about each center, as well as what conclusions could be drawn about nonprofit centers in general.

The first organization in which I became a participant observer was the Puerto Rican Center. During 1994–1995, I volunteered at the Center and collected field notes. After 2 months, I was invited to run on a slate for the election of new board members and became an elected member of the board of directors. Consequently, I was able to receive permission to audiotape the monthly meetings as the recording secretary and as part of my field research. In addition, I received permission to videotape one prominent event for the center, the 1994 Annual Dinner Dance.

To illustrate the boundary of this organization, the Puerto Rican Center's mission statement includes the following line: "To pursue and establish collaborative efforts with other organizations addressing the needs of the Puerto Rican and Spanish-speaking communities" (PRC, 1995, p. 1). Similarly, their vision statement describes the center as existing in order "to promote community involvement and foster leadership development, to meet the diverse social and economic needs of a growing community by providing comprehensive services and to act as an advocate in shaping and influencing the issues that affect our people." That is, what is defined is not just the Puerto Rican Center, but also the larger community that is being served. This definition helps us to understand the organization as inclusive of those people in the community that it serves.

The second organization I examined is a community Family Center (from 2000–2002), which was founded 20 years ago under the auspices of a local psychiatric outpatient clinic as a resource for parents and their children. In particular, the center offers a site for daily drop-ins by parents and caregivers of young children, support groups for new parents, monthly educational workshops for parents, and classes for children in art, music, science, computers, Spanish, and French.

I first became acquainted with the Center when I enrolled my 6-month-old child in a movement class there. One had to become a paid member in order to take a class, and as a member (or past member), one receives newsletters from the Center. Two years after my first acquaintance, I responded to a call that was posted in the newsletter asking any interested parent to contact the director about becoming a new board member. At that time, I inquired about the requirements for board membership and was told to attend the next board meeting in order to stand for election. The board members consented to participate in a research study and elected me to the board as the recording secretary. This role gave me legitimate organizational access to record audio and video of the meetings that I used to produce the meeting minutes and for the purpose of research.

Nuanced Membership

The three main goals of this volume are to demonstrate that (1) what it means to be an organization (whether for-profit or not-for-profit) is integrally related to membership; (2) communication (both spoken and written) *members* organizational participants; and (3) communicating as members creates the *social* categories of organizations. In order to describe membership and the way it works in organizations today, I cover five key areas: Becoming a Member; The Context for Membership; Maintaining Membership; Inscribing Membership; and Changes in Membership. These areas were selected in order to both cover typical, key areas of organizational communication[20] scholarship as well as to demonstrate the process of "membering." That is, these areas represent both researcher, as well as member categories, for activities engaged in within organizations.

The areas are chronologically sequenced. That is, becoming a member is the first concern because it is the first task that must be accomplished by researchers or other new participants with an organization. Once one becomes a member, being able to recognize the context, continuing to participate as a member, using and recognizing membership in written documents and sustaining changes are enacted throughout one's organizational affiliation. Sometimes changes result in the cessation of membership (as an employee or volunteer) and this terminal phase re-orients members and soon-to-be nonmembers to the boundaries of membership.

Membership occurs in moments of interaction. I have captured such moments of organizational life and presently describe them.

Chapter 1

Becoming a Participant/ Becoming a Member

Becoming a member differs from becoming a participant. In this chapter, the process of gaining access as a researcher[21] is used as a metaphor for understanding the process of becoming an organizational member. In order to demonstrate how members treat nonmembers or potential members, examples from my own participant-observation research among community center organizations are used. These data demonstrate not only my own entrance into the setting, but also how other newcomers are greeted and treated by members.

First, let me describe the process of gaining access for my work with each community center. In the first, the Puerto Rican Center (PRC), I telephoned the Director to request a meeting to discuss my research. He asked me to meet him and talk in person. On arriving at the old Victorian building that housed the center, I proceeded into the Director's office. The Assistant Director was already in the room and the Director introduced me to him. After sitting at the table with them, I described my research as examining communication by looking at interpersonal interaction. The Director asked me several questions about my knowledge of the media and after a very brief conversation, I was given permission to volunteer twice a week at the center in order to help them with their "communication." After about 1 month of volunteering twice per week, I was asked if I would agree to be nominated on a slate for new board members. I agreed. Subsequently, the entire slate of nominees was elected by the membership. At our first meeting to determine offices, I was elected as recording secretary. Everyone knew about my research and agreed that I could continue to take field notes as well as audio record the monthly board meetings for purposes of writing the minutes, as well as conducting my research.

Several years later, after having moved to another city in the Northeast, I read an advertisement in a family center's newsletter requesting board members. I telephoned the Director to inquire if one could conduct research while being on the board. The Director suggested that I attend the next board meeting to ask the other board members that question. I did attend the next meeting whereby I sat and listened as the meeting was being conducted. At the end of the meeting, when the time came to talk about open positions, I was asked if I was interested in joining the board. At this time, I described my research project as examining how decisions are made between members of boards of directors. Those present said it sounded like it was compatible. I was then elected to the board and subsequently, elected as secretary of the board. In this position, everyone agreed that I could use an audio-recorder to take minutes, as well as for my own research purposes.

Although both of my stories about gaining access are similar from a mechanical point of view, there were features of what I later came to call "membership" that could be glimpsed during these first encounters. Two of these membership features related to the salient characteristics of the centers themselves—ethnicity and gender. During the PRC nomination conversation, when asked if I would agree to join the slate, I was told that the board was looking for new board members who were young and professional. I asked directly if my not being Puerto Rican would matter. I was informed that not everyone is Puerto Rican; the Assistant Director was Mexican and because I was Mexican American, that made me Hispanic. This answer provided two possible rationales—either I shared a common generic ethnicity, or relatively little importance was placed on being from Puerto Rico or Puerto Rican.[22] I was told that as long as I was interested, that was what was most important for my being included as a member on the slate.[23] For this reason, I seemed able to pass as an acceptable board candidate.

In the second center, ethnicity and gender were not topics of conversation per se, but features of the interaction that were noticeable. There were two of us present who attended the meeting specifically in order to find out about joining the board—one male and one female. When we arrived prior to the meeting and encountered the male president of the board, we were told that the other members were mostly female. I do not think either of us was surprised to learn about this since the center itself was a "family center" and we often hear that women schedule many of their children's activities.

Social categories, such as ethnicity and gender, may be present and able to be identified. However, the salience of these categories for the participants is difficult to determine by beginning with these researcher-defined categories. What these two moments of gaining access demonstrated most was the initial moments in organizational life whereby membership is conferred. Rather than take membership as a given based on the accident of being born Latina, membership is an interactional accomplishment created among participants in organizations that determine who participates and how individuals are or will come to be regarded. This is especially true of organizations that have deemed themselves as "cultural centers" (promoting an ethnic culture or the family).

Certainly, through the process of "gaining access," I was able to become a participant. This participation was conferred initially through talk. The official way that board membership was established was through "a vote." In the PRC, this "vote" came during an annual membership meeting, whereby hands were raised to accomplish the act of voting in the slate. In the second case, the President of the Family Center (FC) board told us at that meeting that by our interest and the act of attending the meeting, we were members (although later I learned that the official way of inducting new board members is by a ballot vote that is requested via the newsletter sent to all members). These organizational acts created the opportunities to participate and held some of the features that make "membership" a relevant category. These early interactions indicate that members have processes that they create, with varying levels of formality, for deciding who is able to become an organizational member.

Membership Labels, Address and Reference

How do new participants become members? The first act is labeling. After being voted in, a participant takes on the social role of "board member." This role title can thereafter be used as a term of address. Becoming a new member is a moment in organizational life usually experienced just after interviews and hiring. For board members, it occurs after the election process. It is often during one's first meeting, or interaction with other members, that membership is conferred through reference and address. In these instances of interaction, communicative acts are coordinated, and membership is or isn't accomplished.

Distinguishing Members

Membership is often indicated by a designated label used for particular categories of members. Before coming to moments of address, the newly elected board member begins to recognize that she is in a category that is in distinction to another, very prominent, and essential category, that of "staff" member. For instance, within PRC board meetings, members indicate two classes of participants, "board members" and "staff persons" (also see Rudd, 1995; Schwartzman et al., 1978). Referring to a class of participants, rather than an individual participant, further delineates the category of member (see Sacks 1989):

```
450.  RM:    I, personally, I don't think it should be a st--, board member's
451.         responsibility and we all get busy in our jobs and I understand
452.  (4.5)
453.  SH:    so, are you saying, R that a staff person should be in here?
454.  RM:    yeah, I gotta follow the lead of the Executive Director on that, um,
455.         and then again, I don't know how the chair, I mean I've been in a position
456.         trying to be the recording secretary and participate in a meeting, you
457.         really can't do both, um, that's why I would suggest that a staff person be
```

458. here, but if the Executive Director doesn't feel that he wants, wants a
459. *staff people* to see the business of the corporation, even though I think
460. we're subject to the open meeting law, um. (April board meeting)[24]

In this segment, two classes of participants are labeled—"board members" and "staff person/people." Sacks (1995) has noted that often *two* classes are set in opposition to one another. This seems to occur in this segment. The board members, and tasks for which board members can properly take responsibility, are set in contrast to activities that staff can and, it is argued, should perform.

Interestingly, the only "staff" member present is the "Executive Director."[25] As RM states, it is the Executive Director's role to decide if "he wants" the staff to be present at the board meetings. Some other responsibilities (pragmatic actions with normative rules) of board members were discussed during other board meetings. Board members *should* "make . . . decision[s]"; give "some suggestions"; "stay on top of this" (getting sponsors for the festival); and "look at the numbers, scrutinize them" (instances from the May board meeting); "take it upon themselves to contact these people"; "get the support for the center"; "raise 'x' amount of dollars"; and "make the effort" (instances from April board meeting). One member's responsibility becomes generalized to a responsibility of the entire group.

In contrast, "staff" is described as an entity in a certain close relationship to the Executive Director. They are characterized as "his" staff, indicating the Executive Director as their boss. For example, "staff" are referred to as something that the Executive Director *has*, as illustrated by the possessive pronoun "his" (line 150).

149. HT: I want to, before we go any further, to thank the
150. Executive Director and *his* staff for sending stuff out
151. [LG: yeah that was very nice] like we talked about last time. (May meeting)

"Staff" are also described as something that the "board" has (see January meeting, line 423, and April meeting, line 495, 416). The staff is talked about as people who are a possession of the Executive Director as well as the "board." Yet, the Executive Director, "JG" was, at times, described as "staff" as in the following example:

376. HT: *JG*
377. EG: I don't think you can
378. A: cause he's *staff.* (January meeting)

Rather than simply asserting that the 13-member Board of Directors define the direction, goals, and tone of the organization, the board and staff's responsibilities were described, asserted, and contested by members. In fact, what it means to be a board member is, in part, juxtaposed with what it means to be a staff person. That is, although some duties and responsibilities of board members are described, they are also set in contrast to the duties of the staff. Both the board and staff are always implicated in descriptions about what either is supposed to be doing.

Merely describing group categories is not the only way that membership is accomplished. As Sequeira (1993) has demonstrated, the use of personal address in introductions and greetings is another way to detail the relationships between certain classes of participants (such as clergy, staff, and congregation). Likewise, individuals are assigned a group membership by the way they are addressed.

Addressing Individual Members

One of the first noticeable titles a member may hold is one that I obtained shortly after being "voted in" as a board member. I was elected as the recording secretary. In this role, I began to notice that the way that other participants addressed one another designated membership. For instance, at the PRC, a board member addressed the new board president by saying, "Mr. Chairman." This title seemed to be very formal.[26] Consider the following example that occurred during the January 1995 board meeting:

54.	HT:	everyone looks cheery as usual
55.	PL:	good morning *H*,
56.		good to see you
57.	LG:	good morning *Mr. President*
58.	HT:	thank you
59.		I like that
60.		oh, great one
61.	PL:	great one?
62.		you've been president how long
63.		unbelievable
64.	AB:	that happened really quick
65.	HT:	the next day, um

The first item to note is the greeting with first name (line 55). The next person to greet the same person changes the address form from the familiar, informal first name to gender marker and title, "Mr. President" (line 57).[27] HT affirms this response and then tries to take it to a higher level "oh, great one." This is contested in the next line, "great one?" (line 61).

One interpretation of this example is that the President's formal role is known by others, but that the use of the title in this case implicates other members as *not* the president. This form of address is an exaggeration that demonstrates that titles are more proper than first names in this setting. It also may indicate simply that members have different roles from one another, and they can be labeled as such by other members. Another interpretation is that by using what might be called respectful behavior, the participants make note that they are not merely peers who all have first names, but rather, some participants have roles that create a hierarchical arrangement. Prior to the elections of the board members and their positions, HT and LG spoke to each other on a first-name basis. After the elections, this sequence occurs and demonstrates the change of positions. The elections then created an opportunity to alter address terms and actually functioned to changed the members' roles and their relationships to one another.

However, membership is conferred not only by referencing categories or changing address forms, but one can demonstrate membership by enacting it. Another common way this is achieved is through introductions.

Introductions

In the Family Center, whenever a visitor or potential new board member attended a board meeting, the sequence of introductions was always conducted in a similar manner. The president (or co-president)[28] would indicate that introductions should proceed around the room and would give an example. She would state her name, her reason for first coming to the center, how long she had been at the center, and her child(ren)'s name and/or age(s).

It is the placement of introductions at the outset of the meeting that begins to set the tone of the meeting. Furthermore, introductions provide an opportunity for participants to learn about each other's background and interests in the center. For even if participants "knew" one another before the meeting, how they introduce themselves during and for any one meeting draws others' attention to particular features of themselves, including their current interests. Finally, in the process of making introductions everyone learns how their comments will "be heard" by one another.

During a board retreat, JS, the Co-President, instructed board members by saying:

17. ...and introduce ourselves to each other. Say a little about who we are and what
18. brings you to the Family Center and if there is anything specific that you feel you
19. bring to Family Center like interest, goals and talents. I'll start, I'm Jennifer
20. Stevenson, co-president with Michael Fumigali. And hmm, I guess ((laughs)) I don't
21. remember how long I have been on the board, I have been on the board for 4 years
22. and I started coming to Family Center when I moved into the neighborhood. I have
23. four children, it is a real community for parents and children. Once I started coming
24. here it was pretty clear, I knew I wanted to help out. In terms of what I bring

25. ((laughs)), I guess parenting experience. I like working with the many functions that
26. we have (.) especially Spring Fling and Super Saturdays. It is something that I really
27. enjoy ...

In lines 17–19, JS set up the model for introductions by labeling the activity as "introduce ourselves" (line 17). She specified that participants should include "what brings you to the Family Center" (lines 17–18), as well as what each "brings," such as "interest, goals, and talents" (line 19). She then demonstrated how to make an introduction and her example included her tenure with the board, "4 years" (line 21); her reasons for "coming to" the center were her "four children" and "moving into the neighborhood" (lines 22–23); her specific talents were her "parenting experience"; and her interest was working on the "functions" that the center hosts (lines 25–26).[29]

After giving her introduction, JS gave all of the other participants an opportunity to be involved in group introductions. A board member started this process, the Director of the center sitting next to her then followed in a similar manner, and it went around in a consecutive, clockwise order. Each speaker spoke without interruptions. During the introductions, each person said a little about herself stating what brought her to the Family Center, how long she had been there, her talents and goals for the center, and the particular concerns she had for the center. Some of the participants mentioned their professional backgrounds, their children's ages, skills, and interests. By doing so, participants demonstrated that "talk is not just talk, but rather the mode and medium through which the organization [or group] is constituted and reconstituted" (Boden, 1994, p. 202).

Although this segment illustrates how a member formally structured introductions, the pattern itself was already established and prevalent at the monthly board meetings. Introductions were common when persons came to the meeting after an extended absence from the Center (as in the case below) or when a new person was interested in possibly joining the board. The example in the following dialogue begins with the simple word, "introductions." In this segment, we can hear members producing similar kinds of statements as in the example above, including the age of their child, living in the neighborhood and an activity in the Family Center in which they participate (even when they have to add that information after their main speaking turn) and without being prompted to do so.

1. MF: does everyone know
2. F & J: introductions
3. A: No
4. MF: maybe we should do that
5. B: hi J
6. A: my son is 17 $^1/_2$ and my daughter who came with me first to Family Center to do cooking is now 15, she was 2 at the time

22   Chapter 1

7.   B: my son is 15 I think we came when he was 3 weeks old
8.   MF: [hh hh hh]
9.   A: we went into a mommy and baby class and I still meet with my mommy support class
10. MF: [wow]
11. B: [we started in 1984
12. B: [MF: great] it shrunk. but we still meet
13. A: [hh hh hh]
14. MF: that's great, thank you And J why don't you introduce yourself
15. JC: yea, my name is JC. I live in the neighborhood and I am an attorney for a firm[30]
16. MF: [a small one]
17. JC:
             [yea,
18. JC: It's getting larger and larger, um
19. JC: And um I've volunteered at the Spring Fling last year because I wanted to get more involved with the organization, and um, be here, I'm here to [hh hh] get more involved
20. MF: thank you for coming
21. .
22. .
23. C: I have an 11 year old too
24. C: I live on. . . . (April 2000 FC meeting)

This set of introductions was much more interactive and featured turn-overlap[31] more than the formal introductions at the retreat whereby one person spoke for an extended time without interruption before moving on to the next speaker.

    Here multiple speakers construct the introductions. Line 2 has both F and J saying "introductions" suggesting that they begin presently, which does in fact occur. In line 5, a first name greeting is given. Making reference to another member by first name[32] is done in line 14. In this case, it is a pre-empted introduction of JC, who continues by stating her first and last name in line 15. Children and their ages are specified (lines 6, 7, 23). A child is implied with the word, "we" in line 9. The importance of living in the neighborhood is demonstrated in lines 15 and 24, as is participating in Family Center activities (lines 6, 9, 19: cooking, mommy and baby classes, and Spring Fling respectively).

    In this instance, the male Co-President speaks initially (line 1), then two female members initiate introductions. Later the male Co-President requests an introduction (line 14) of the other members after the former members completed their self-introductions. In this way, he enacts his role of President by directing subsequent action (even though the pattern of introductions had been established, the sequence of who speaks next was open).

Unlike at the PRC, in all of the Family Center introductions, no one uses a title to introduce themselves or to refer to others. Rather, the use of first names prevails. Furthermore, one does not hear in Family Center introductions or discussions the distinct membership categories of board and staff. However, each center creates membership categories (by introduction, address and reference) and establishes member positions (and actions) in relation to one another:

- Board with staff
- President with Executive Director
- Parent with Child(ren)
- Member with Center

In all of these ways, membership is indicated. Individual participants are noted and valued differently in each center. Accordingly, patterns of doing membership differ. For instance, member categories can pit roles and relationships (being a mother vs. a board member) or members as juxtaposed against others in the larger set (staff vs. board). Although these two examples of introductions seem to demonstrate that roles and membership categories are synonymous, examining additional conversations is warranted.

Initial Membership Categories

When a person becomes a participant in a group, whether or not that person is a researcher, one finds that the rules that induct that person into the group imply certain things about the group itself. The process of voting in new board members demonstrates that the board members of these two organizations value the rule that mandates a vote before assuming office. This early norm formally establishes who may be talked about and to, henceforth in the category of board member.

Not only does membership imply group associations, but members themselves often refer to members in groupings. These member categories form a subset of the larger category of members. Whereas in some ethnographic studies these subsets have been referred to with labels referencing a teacher as a "lady" or "Mrs. Ganin" (Philipsen, 1990/1991) or workers who called distinct groups, "the movers," "the secure," and "the paper-movers" (Carbaugh, 1988), whichever categories are used by the members themselves indicates those that are most salient to that organization (such as "board" and "staff").

The act of addressing individuals first by name and then through a role title helps to indicate the importance of roles for these members. Finally, making introductions demonstrates additional features of membership that are valued, such as having a child, living in the neighborhood and taking part in the organizations activities. Sacks (1995) speaks at length about the use of introductions to create membership categories (e.g., see Lecture 04.a, 04.b, and 4). From introductions, he notes several points, such as: the importance of sequence, who is being introduced by whom and to whom; how members know how to proceed; seating order plays a role; multiparty conversations prompt consideration to who is speaking and who is not spoken to; and what is *not* happening may be very important. Significantly, Sacks (1995) draws the relationship between introductions and address and membership. He notes that introduction not only "do naming" (p. 289), but also give instructions for how to address someone. In addition, he notes that the information given during introductions is crucial for the kind of "identification" the person makes (p. 284)—that indicates the member category to which a person belongs.

All of these forms are ways of doing membership. We are beginning to learn the nuanced ways that organizational members create their sense of membership, as well as how they organize themselves. By first finding how participants create members by labeling individuals and groups, we can then move to examine specific speaking situations, such as meetings, to learn more about how participants enact membership through decisions for which they are held accountable by other members.

Before coming to individual decisions, though, special event meetings that foreground commonality are described. Speech events, rituals and context form the core analytic apparatus to examine the boundaries that extend beyond the organization itself, to its external constituents. The context for these centers as "community centers" is actually created through member talk.

Chapter 2

Membership in a Community Context

Both of the organizations examined held a special event that commemorated their center and the work they were doing within the community. These events took much planning and occupied much talk during the regularly scheduled monthly board meetings. Although the events in each center had many similarities in terms of form and function (they were both gala, anniversary celebrations[33]), each event also seemed to create an opportunity for speakers to contextualize the work of the center within a larger community. In this chapter, I explore the way that talk at these events seems to focus on what each center labels "community" and conclude with a discussion about how this talk functions in each center, both as a way to demonstrate the values that the organization holds as well as to forge tighter connections and relationships to people outside the specific organization that creates an extended sense of "membership."

After briefly providing details about each center's event, I demonstrate how members speak about their communities. This talk seems to provide a context that is one way of characterizing the nature of nonprofit centers. Social interaction takes place within a context that is created through conversations as well as reified in subsequent conversations. How the context is talked into being includes implications relevant for members of each center, such as being Puerto Rican or being a neighbor. These specific features of membership are part of the community context that can be heard in talk at each center.

PRC's Annual Dinner Dance

Each year, the PRC hosts a formal dinner dance event at a banquet facility[34] in order to showcase the center's accomplishments.[35] Center members are invited, as are other prominent members of the community, including legislators and educators. Some of the prominent guests are invited to deliver brief remarks. The order of events is outlined in a printed program that is given to each attendee on arrival at the event and includes messages from the President of the board of directors and the Executive Director. Each program provides details of the year's events and advertisements from local businesses. Although these events are scheduled for a particular time, participants arrive[36] and depart, as they will.

During all of the speeches at the 18th anniversary dinner and within 5 year's worth of the printed programs that were given to guests of each dinner, I found that the word "community" was used more frequently than any other. The repetition of the term community seemed to serve a vital function in creating the context for actions within the center. Consider the following two instances from two dinner speakers.

228. SH: my hope is I can represent the children as well as the Puerto Rican
229.   community of Springfield...
304. MM: Puertoriqueños as a community have advanced for the first time...

These two instances illustrate the way that two different speakers reference "community." In the first utterance by SH, "community" is used to refer specifically to the locally bound, ethnic community of Puerto Ricans. In the second utterance by MM, "community" becomes a broader concept that refers to all those who are Puerto Rican, seemingly outside of narrow geographic boundaries. In these instances we begin to see evidence that the meanings of community can be either local or general, but that the term itself somehow connotes and is used to refer to PRC group membership.

By using the term *community*, participants of this celebratory event seem to be claiming membership in the center. For example, when phrases such as, "Puerto Rican Community," "service to Latino community," and "crime in our community,"[37] are uttered and heard, they are part of the symbolic resources (Fitch, 1998) that members use to create the context (and text) of this organization.

In order to be heard as a member, participants not only refer to "community," but they include themselves by speaking about the Puerto Rican community as "our community." By using the pronoun "our" with community, as in the value of "our community," participants speak themselves into a membership relationship with those who also speak by referring to "our community" (for a similar point, see Carbaugh, Gibson, & Milburn, 1997).

Community as Metaphor

At times, members discuss the physical location of "community," such as the town of "Springfield." We can hear such phrases as "placenames" (Basso, 1990; Schegloff, 1972a, 1972b) with deeper cultural meaning. On another occasion, the center was described as located in the "north end." To make reference to such a place is to know not only the geographic location, but that there is a large Puerto Rican population in this part of the city. Further, it includes a lower socioeconomic population than other parts of the city. Therefore, when the "north end" is mentioned, participants take care to state that the Puerto Rican community is not contained or constrained by this location, nor does the center only service the needs of people located there. Although the center is physically located in the north end,[38] when I spoke to participants they took the opportunity to describe the Puerto Rican community as extending beyond the physical boundaries of the "north end." Members take care to assert the importance of the concept "community" as extending beyond the physical location of the center, and as inclusive of other potential members who may live anywhere. By speaking as such, the Center is not identified with only potential negative connotations that some may associate with such a location.

During this annual event, members invoke a communal term, *community*, not simply to refer to a small geographic area where the Puerto Rican Center is located; rather, "community" extends beyond this spatial boundary into an inclusive social sphere where all Latinos are members. Furthermore, based on the ways "community" is used grammatically, we can hear "community" used as a container metaphor by members who describe it as "having" needs, issues, and so forth. A container metaphor has been used elsewhere to describe "self," (Carbaugh 1988; 1993; Lakoff & Johnson 1980,[39] Shotter 1985, 1989). Containers hold something. They hold something one *has* (similar possessive feature as "our"). They can be temporary or permanent. They contain that which might otherwise not be contained: things might leak out, get out, and have to be put back in. Some containers are fragile and can break. Finally, a container metaphor implies that it is right (moral) that things be contained. In this case, "community" contains this nonprofit organization.

The spoken "community" contains the groups' (PRC) identity.[40] The "community" refers to members being contained by it as well as being contained within the space of "community." This metaphor extends to the container's consequences. If the container breaks or is damaged, the contents (i.e., our members) suffer.

Community Actions

During the PRC dinner I attended, the keynote speaker focused on the community in a way that was consistent with the theme: "Investing in Our Youth." In his address, he used parallel structure to substantiate the relationship between community, its members and "problems." He said,

342. We, in the final analysis, will be held to blame,
343. for every young member of our community

344. who doesn't go on to higher education,
345. and is denied the opportunity;
346. for every young member of our community,
347. who wants to work, but can't find a job;[41]
348. for every young member of our community,
349. who is taken from us forever,
350. because of the plague of AIDS,
351. which can be prevented,
352. but against which our young are not now protected,
353. and are not being educated.

Blame falls to the whole community, as in "we will be to blame." All of us, the community as a whole and not individual members, are held accountable. When the speaker discusses the future, he does so by using the collective "we," which includes the speaker and the audience in "blamable actions." However, the reverse can be true too. In the community, it is individuals (un-named as such) who can be responsible for the "problems in our community." Because they remain un-named or unidentified (as apart from community), they cannot be blamed, or pointed to as responsible "individuals."[42]

One extreme implication his statements suggest is that in a problem-ridden future, the community itself may cease to exist. The young members of community who are not receiving help for the current problems will not grow up to be adult members of the community. This would lead to a disintegration of community, and all that would remain would be "individuals." As such, the group would be blamed because it was not able to keep the community together.

Speakers, who use *community* in their remarks, position themselves as one who can claim that this is "our" community, implicating him/herself as a member. The keynote speaker made use of the phrase "our community" in this way (lines 343, 346, 348), even though he was from another state. By claiming membership, one also claims responsibility for the community as a whole. When the keynote speaker says "we will be to blame," he affirms the values of a community as a whole, comprised of individuals who are parts of this whole, and that service and work to help the community is warranted when the parts of our community, such as "youth," are not being well served or "protected." The social sanctions for breaking the community norms are uncertain, besides placing "blame." If "we" fail "our community," we can be identified, named as such, and then blamed. Given the inclusive norm for naming individuals as members within the community, rather than separate or apart from the community, such a community can easily become "broken" by problems that are detrimental to its very existence.

As demonstrated here, center members and guest speakers reference community. When members speak in such a way, they are invoking several nuances of meaning: community is an inclusive space that extends beyond geographic boundaries; community is a way for people to stand together and not be marked as separate individuals—community contains; community has "needs" and "problems" that its members seek to address; community includes a sensed ideal towards which current actions should move, and be assessed. As understood this way, "community" is a symbol that provides a frame for understanding the activities that occur within this Puerto Rican Center.

By noting how speakers during this annual dinner event make use of the term *community*, we learn more about how speakers (members) create through their utterances, a sense of what community is, reinforce notions of what community has been, and speaking into the future about what community can be. These senses of creating context through talk are all present in these instances. It is interesting to note that other dinner speakers used the same term, albeit in slightly different ways.

Family Center Gala Anniversary Event

Although the Family Center does not hold an *annual* event to celebrate its accomplishments, it did host a "20th Anniversary Gala" to celebrate this milestone.[43] This fundraising event was held to celebrate the anniversary of the Center by honoring several persons who had been key figures in its development. This event was held in the Jewish Synagogue Hall across the street from FC. It was held in the evening (6:30–8:30 p.m.) and many people had arrived prior to stated starting time, lining up outside the hall. The event ended promptly 2 hours later as stated in the invitations issued. After a short time when everyone was still arriving, paying admission, getting name tags, drinks, and hors d'oeuvres, the President of the board of directors stepped up on stage and began his role as master of ceremonies. He made brief remarks and then introduced each honored guest and government officials who spoke to those assembled.

Although not used as frequently or as extensively as in the PRC, "community" was a term that was repeated by nearly every FC speaker. Consider some of the following instances heard:

SD: spirit in a community
P: Part of the community
DLS: Your commitment to your own community
R: fight for his community

By speaking of "community," each speaker placed the Family Center's activities in context or in relations to the idea of community.

Location of Community

After examining all of the instances of "community" that were used, the most common way was to use it as a term referencing people living near the Center. For instance, the keynote speaker, DLS referred to the community with second-person, possessive label: "your own community." Some speakers claimed to belong to "our community," and yet other speakers described a place where they did not belong, "your community."

The container metaphor can be demonstrated by those expressions that include the word "in" the community. During the event, speakers used such phrases as, "the people *in* the community." In this way, "community" contains people. This community is a place called the *neighborhood*, rather than an ethnic designation referencing participants (as in the PRC).

As MC, the President of the board of directors first referenced the neighbors. The Director of Family Center, who was the first honoree, also mentioned that it was good to see "neighbors." Subsequent speakers also talked about neighbors or the neighborhood. One elected official, SD talked about living in the "neighborhood," and described another government official who helped the Center as living "several neighborhoods away." The importance of physically locating participants in geographic space was further indicated when the city was mentioned by name when the MC introduced the second two honorees as "born and raised" in the city. Clearly the location and label of "neighbor" or "neighborhood" are important descriptors of this "community."

The place or location of community became very significant in a recent struggle with the mayor over an eviction notice that tenants received because the mayor has decided to use the space for a homeless shelter. It was during this "struggle" over their lease in the building they had been housed in for the past 20 years that the term *community* seemed to become the most relevant. In local newspaper articles from 1998–1999, several of the references to community are explicitly related to one occupant in the building, that is a "Community Board." In these articles, the Family Center is described as a "neighborhood center," "a not-for-profit organization," or as one of many "community organizations." As in the speeches during the event, when talking about the Family Center, community is described as a neighborhood and community members as neighbors.

Community Struggles to Serve

Several speakers referred to this struggle that the Center and community organizations within the same building waged with the mayor. This struggle was the one specific event that brought members of the community, specifically those living in the neighborhood, together to "fight" on behalf of the Center in order to keep it open so that it could "serve" its community members.

Membership in a Community Context

During this celebratory event, the person who talked about this sense of "community" most was a government official, SD. He was serving on the City Council representing the district. As such, he spoke from a sense of both geographic location and as a person who lived and represented others within that area. He described the community's "spirit" that could be felt during his "fight" with the mayor on behalf of the community.

1. SD: (.) I'll do three things.
2. One, I'll do what we're here for, celebrate 20 wonderful years of a terrific program and all the people who've ever been associated with it or participated in it or gave to it or showed up to one of its events. Second, thing a bit of old business, just a bit of old business, ya know the fight that we had over 123 Basic Street, wasn't a fight between two personalities, I disagree with the mayor often, fight for a spirit in a community that believes in those programs—for seniors and kids, for the mentally ill, for our community.
3. (.) it was about a community that gives back and believes in giving back. Kids are suffering less (.) law and changes made (.) but our community is benefiting more. I think it was an important reflection of how wonderful this community is ((audience applause)).

Within this segment, we find this government official including himself in reference to the community. Although he varies from using "a community" to "our community" he does locate himself as a member by reiterating his actions with others, "the fight *we* had." In this speech, community is a very specific place that is geographically located. To be a member, then, one either had to "be associated," "participate," or "show up" to an event (segment 2) in order to belong to this "wonderful community" (segment 3).

During the Family Center "struggle" the following actions occurred,

- "fight for his community"
- "forced his ego on this community"
- "community rallied around him"

From the local news articles, the action of "fighting" City Hall was a momentary response to an eviction notice. However, once the eviction was rescinded, the need to "fight" was no longer a necessary or permissible action to take. Likewise, the need to "rally" around was only a temporary need that had passed once circumstances changed.

The speeches given during this celebration exemplify two significant features of community for members of the FC. The first is the location of community in a neighborhood, and the second are the actions taken on behalf of those the community serves. The population that the Family Center and other agencies within 123 Basic Street *serve* was described as "seniors and kids, for the mentally ill, for our community (SD, line 2). Being a recipient of service is one way to affiliate with the Center.

The anniversary speakers may have used this past situation in order to recreate the sense of unity that joined participants together in the successful struggle. In fact, many of those assembled for this dinner were those who underwent the trial and survived it together, as a community. The anniversary would not have been possible, had the Family Center been evicted. However, this struggle in the recent past was not the genesis of the Center.

Community History

In her account of the genesis of the Family Center, the co-guest of honor, MS told a story about her attendance at a conference that distributed a "Community Mental Health" report from the U.S. Government. In it, she found the advice that prompted her to begin the Family Center. She stated, "every community mental health center should have a parenting center attached to it." The idea that the Family Center was historically related to the "community mental health" movement prompted me to examine the origins of this word.[44]

According to two online accounts,[45] the term *community care* was first used in 1957 in the Percy Report. "Community mental health" seems to have been further promoted in the late 1970s in several documents and policy changes—which apparently prompted the services that were created in the building that houses the Family Center.

The Percy Report (1957) itself contrasted community care with hospital care. It used the phrase "in the community" to refer to care that was provided outside of hospitals. This type of care was preferred and advocated over care in isolated mental hospitals.

The next major advancement in this movement was Enoch Powell's (1961) Water Tower Speech. In this speech, he is credited with laying out the "full scope" for community care and services that should be provided for the mentally ill. This speech was given as the opening remarks of a conference of the National Association for Mental Health. As Minister of Health, Powell described how his plan would alter psychiatric services.

In the book, *The Myth of Mental Illness*, Szasz (1974) argued that the perception of "mental illness" is as much defined by the milieu in which the behavior occurs as it is by the signs and symptoms manifested in said behavior. This book was part of a growing body of literature redefining how mental health services were understood.

Later the National Mental Health Association (NMHA) would play a major role.

In 1980, NMHA's 3-year leadership role in raising grass-roots support and cooperation with the federal government resulted in the development and passage of the Mental Health Systems Act of 1980. The Act fostered the continued growth of America's Community Mental Health Centers which allow individuals with mental illnesses to remain in their home *communities* with minimal hospitalization. (http://www.nmha.org/about/history.cfm, paragraph 7, emphasis added)

These reports indicate that *community care* was a term specifically denoting mental health care. Because the Family Center began as a part of a mental health facility (and still resides in the same building with a "community care" clinic), the term *community*, meaning not in a hospital, is a very different, but important referent for long time members of this organization.

Discussion

The examples just noted illustrate how anniversary dinner participants use words to describe themselves, the centers, and all of those people associated their cause. Unlike the previous chapter about individual role labels and categories for members, the labels in this chapter link individuals into a larger unit.

There are three methodological terms that can help us understand how this is accomplished. In this discussion, I elaborate how this member talk is conducted through a *ritual* to highlight *community* that provides a *context* for member discourse and action.

These dinner celebrations are similar in many ways. That they share a look and feel across time and space indicates that these celebrations may be a common way to do things in organizations.[46] There are two terms that are used within organizational studies to describe patterned ways of doing things: *rite* and *ritual*. Whereas Deal and Kennedy (1982) do not differentiate between the two, Trice and Beyer (1984, 1993) describe ritual as merely a routine practice and use the term rite to refer to more formalized transitional phases (e.g. rites of passage). Knuf (1993) counters this claim and seeks to reintroduce ritual as the more preferred term among organizational researchers, such that ritual refers to a formalized practice that demonstrates either commonality or disintegrating relationships. Although Philipsen (1987) uses ritual in a way that Knuf describes as a trope: the communal use of symbols in a patterned way that celebrates a sacred object, Leeds-Hurwitz (2002) articulates a more precise definition: the intentional, purposeful, predictable structure to reaffirm social bonds, transform participants, and mark and maintain tradition.[47]

When members attend the celebratory dinner events, they seem to be performing a ritual. Within both anniversary celebrations, participants purposefully act in ways that affirm social bonds. In these celebrations, participants use a discourse that coalesces around a symbol that stands for group cohesion, "community." Therefore, rituals form the link from practice to interpretation.

The term *community*, although used by participants as a symbol, also has theoretical implications as indicated in the introductory chapter. A speech community is one that describes participants who share common linguistic features (Hymes, 1974). However, the term has been used by EC scholars more recently to label those who share a common geographic space (see Milburn, 2004). The term *speech community* is useful because it describes the boundaries of any one particular group that is dependent on the ways it speaks that separates it from any other group.[48]

In these two centers, the term *community center* is a governmental definition, but also refers to the physical location and the actions that are associated with the people so designated. Each could be thought of as a speech community in that their emphasis and the value of "community" is distinct. Or, both could be considered members of the same speech community of nonprofit organizations because they both engage in this ritual practice of celebrating the accomplishments of the organization. In this case, all of those who participate would be considered part of the nonprofit speech community.[49]

The third theoretical term that might help us to understand this data is *context*. Many times, context is used in communication models as the circle within which communication takes place (Pearce & Pearce, 2004). *Context* is also a term that has been contested by EC and CA researchers (see Tracy, 1998). Ethnographers of communication consider context to be any additional information that can be used by participants as a conversational resource (Fitch, 1998; Hymes, 1974). Conversation Analysts determine context by limiting their research to a specific interaction and those features that participants indicate are relevant (Hopper & LeBaron, 1998). Heritage (1984) extends this notion by recognizing how words are "doubly contextual" in that they provide a conversational context and become the context for future interaction (as cited in Goodwin & Duranti, 1992).

The speeches made at the dinner events included multiple references to "community." Therefore, by the CA criteria, *community* was a term made relevant by participants. By EC criteria, how "community" was used in other settings, such as board meetings, dinner programs, and local newspapers and historical documents may be relevant to help us learn how the term community was indexed by members.[50] That is, the term itself referred to other information not present in the brief remarks made during the dinners. Therefore, through examining the sequence of these ritual events, finding the symbol community and learning its variants and its past, present, and future meanings for members, demonstrates the context within which membership is enacted.

To summarize, there are four main ways that Center members create community as the context for their actions.

1. Community is a container[51] for ethnicity, gender, and age;
2. Community is a way to link individual interactants in any one event;
3. Community is a resource for membering:
    a. It provides a way for members/speakers to draw on terms that make sense of how participants fit together
    b. It is indexical—a short-hand way to tie together—and when unpacked, it has specific meanings for each organization;
4. Community is a ritual form—it is a way to *do* context

Following from here, we can then move to the everyday, more mundane rituals[52] such as monthly board meetings. These meetings do not celebrate a sacred object *per se*, but do demonstrate patterned practices that also serve a membering function, albeit in a different, less formal way.

Chapter 3

Maintaining Membership Through Meetings[53]

In the context of community, membership is enacted most frequently by engaging in routine activities, such as monthly board meetings. Meetings have been described as the primary activity that creates organizations (Swartzman, 1989). Therefore, meetings are an activity that explicitly implicates organizational identity. It is during meetings that members come together to describe work tasks and talk the organization into being by gaining agreement that the tasks they undertake are worthy, that such tasks are being done in the proper way and by the proper person, and that future tasks should be accomplished in order for the organization to function as it does. By describing the patterned ways board members conduct their meetings, one can begin to gain a sense of how membership is maintained by common, routine interactions that recur at expected intervals.

This chapter demonstrates the way that membership is not only created, but maintained in mundane, organizational meetings. The form that meetings take and the purpose for which members presumably meet—to make decisions—reify the community context in a more day-to-day, ritual form (Hall, 1997) rather than the special form from the previous chapter. In their meeting interactions, members make meaningful particular parts of their organizational identities. For instance, in moments of decision talk, members' statements are judged as sensible or not by other members. These moments illustrate how membership is jointly produced as a reciprocal component of what is often looked at as merely decision-making.[54] Before discussing specific decision-making instances, the shape or form, or some might say the structure, of meetings provides the boundaries of this context for member-talk.

Meeting Sequences and Norms

Serving as a board member to both centers, I came to recognize that how board meetings were conducted progressed along some fairly typical lines.[55] Although a claim can be made that meeting behavior follows Robert's Rules of Order (Patnode, 1989) in its ideal state, not all meeting participants are conversant with such rules, or follow them strictly (Weitzel & Geist, 1998). What seems most typical is the following: a meeting time is set, a majority of participants arrive by the time the meeting is supposed to begin, and the chair calls the meeting to order.[56] Those present approve the minutes from the previous meeting and then proceed with topics that have been noted on an agenda. The director gives some kind of report and often refers members to topics that are most relevant given his or her day-to-day knowledge of the center (also see Carbaugh, 1985).

In both nonprofit centers, the meetings shared similar features, even if one held meetings in the morning and the other, in the evening. For instance, typically meetings at the Family Center were held on a previously determined weeknight, (often a Wednesday or Thursday) and had a starting time of 7:00 or 7:30 p.m. A printed agenda and minutes were distributed by the director at the outset of the meeting. The President[57] usually began the meeting by asking if everyone read the minutes from the previous meeting. Members were given about 1 minute[58] to do so, at which time there was a motion to approve the minutes. The President calls on the Director to give a report. This is a spoken, rather than written report. Her report includes detailed information about the checking and Certificate of Deposit (CD) accounts and any recent events that have transpired during the week, as well as issues that have arisen over staffing or other maintenance issues on which she wants board input. After her report, the Director or President may initiate a discussion of the upcoming events that are listed on the written agenda. This discussion continues until the meeting concludes approximately 2-1/2 hours after it began. Although most members arrive and depart near the stated meeting time, at times, a member or two may arrive late or leave before the meeting has concluded.

This sequence of events was routinely enacted and included typical features. For instance, introductions were made whenever a newcomer attended a meeting. As mentioned in the first chapter, each member of the Family Center introduces him or herself by stating his or her name, the ages of his or her children, and the way he or she first came to the Center. At other times during meetings, participants routinely spoke about topics they had knowledge of or interest in, not waiting to be called on and talking at length until another topic arose. A final recurrent feature of meetings was that the President moderated the meeting by changing topics, often referring to the agenda as a way to move the conversation along. Although there are other patterned ways of speaking during meetings (such as pre, or postmeeting talk), these meeting sequences and turn-taking norms are a common way that organizational membership is created—mainly due to members' own recognition of the importance of these events as central to organizational life.

Meetings as Mundane

Talk at meetings can be mundane and ordinary. There are many activities in which board members engage. Some of these have been characterized by researchers as speech acts, such as to: inform, persuade, elaborate, clarify, agree, disagree, and so on. Based on the mission of most nonprofit organizations, participants themselves are likely to characterize their main activity as fundraising. Some might even say that the ability to maintain membership and organizational status is contingent on raising funds.

Both nonprofit centers in this study held spring events that were the major fundraiser for the centers. Often, much of the talk during the board meetings was topically related to these major fundraisers. Members were often challenged to demonstrate their commitment to the organization by showing how much they were working on the fundraising aspects.

For instance, at PRC, fundraising was frequent board meeting topic. There were several specific episodes that foreground fundraising, such as when we were given a challenge to donate directly when one member pulled out her checkbook and wrote a check to the Center; when we hired a consultant to coordinate the spring event that board members usually coordinated; and when the topic of who has solicited the most donations was raised. At FC, fundraising was salient when we were asked to go to local businesses to find donations for a silent auction; and, when we complained at the retreat that we did not all possess the skills to do this well. In both centers, board members were expected to pay the admission fees to attend the gala anniversary events and to be dues-paying members.

Yet, even though one could say that members fundraise and that meetings are often devoted to discussions about fundraising, the steps that are taken prior to fundraising include decision making. Consider the following instance from the Puerto Rican Center that demonstrates a decision related to fundraising:

> 10. JG: again, you know we *decided* to go that route, because it was in anticipation that the board would be able to *raise* x amount of dollars, I don't know if its 5, 6 thousand dollars that we anticipated that the board could generate, so that when you guys went to the festival, you didn't really have to go to work, you would go there to do public relations. (May meeting)

Although the business literature often describes meetings as the sight where decisions are made, much of the talk during meetings does not take the form that one might typically associate with decision making. In these nonprofit organizations, I found that decision making is not based on large, important problems all the time. More frequently, decisions are made about small matters that are deemed important to the daily functioning of the center. In the following section, I describe several instances whereby board members talk about routine affairs of their centers. During these discussions, some decisions are heard to be made. What is noticeable about the decisions themselves is how much time and space are afforded to each topic given its seemingly trivial importance. To members, what is discussed and decided is not trivialized. Members of these centers do spend time working through the pros and cons of decisions and bring to bear what they consider relevant arguments in favor of any one proposal. After describing several instances of meeting interaction at each Center, I conclude with some thoughts about how the interactions member participants.

FC Decision Making

> 510. MF: There you go, so everyone I hope knows everyone else ... We're gonna skip down and you'll notice also if you've read quickly through the minutes, we did go through quite a bit about the 20th anniversary and *we did make some decisions about* that at the last meeting, so (.5) there are some, other things that we need to do and L has a list. (April 2000 meeting, emphasis added)

As this brief instance demonstrates, decision making is commonly the stated function or goal of meetings. However, according to Schwartzman (1989) and Boden (1994), decisions are rarely made in meetings (also see Weick, 1995). Often, decisions are made in the course of one's workday (often by the director or staff) and it is during meetings that these decisions are described, and then the circumstances, context, and rationale for a particular decision is justified and made meaningful to all participants.

Although a board meeting is commonly understood as the place where decisions are made, if one listens carefully to the talk during the meeting, one discovers that decisions are made on a daily basis and only *reported* during the board meeting. What can be made during meetings are "plans" for the future. Therefore, during his or her report, the Executive Director reports about past, or already made (and possibly enacted) "decisions." In the case of FC, the Director reports about decisions such as grants that were applied for, events that were scheduled, teachers who were hired, and "classes [that] were cancelled" (d.10/01). All of these actions were taken and reported after the fact to the assembled board. During the Director's report, board members may question certain decisions that were made—such as "how much should the organization keep in the checking account?" or even question who is qualified to make such a decision, calling into question the very skills of the person who did make the decision. For example, in the May 2000 FC meeting, during the brief financial report, the following interaction occurred that called into question board member roles and the opportunity for additional volunteers

1. JC: I was actually, the reason I asked, was because I mean, do, do um, is there a financial advisor who advises us?
2. AM: no, I've been treasurer, trying to help with those *decisions,* and personally I'm not that familiar with investments, so I really rely on people at work to tell me what to do, so, um, you know, I think that if someone wanted to, if you wanted to talk about better investments it's something that, I'm not, you know, I know how to really . . .

In this example, the Treasurer (AM) refers to decisions (line 2). This reference indicates that decisions have been made, and the implication is that they have been made outside of board meetings. Given her role as Treasurer, AM explains that she tries to "help with" decisions, but that she is not an expert with investments. JC asked his question (line 1) after the Director gave her financial report; a report that typically includes a summary of the money in checking and CDs. So, although this example does not demonstrate decisions being made, it does demonstrate that decisions are made and then reported about during the meeting. After this sequence, JC goes on to suggest that we invite a financial advisor who might want to volunteer to help the center. AM agrees that this would be a good idea.[59]

At times, decisions are reported as having been made at previous meetings (see lines 10 and 510 above for past-tense references). In order to learn more about how decision making occurs during meetings, one should examine closely an extended meeting interaction during which issues are discussed and votes are taken. The following example from a Family Center meeting illustrates how members talk decisions into being and also implicate themselves as members in the process.

The following lengthy example takes place at the February, 2001 meeting. The written agenda was as follows:

Family Center Board Meeting—February 7, 2001[60] Agenda:
Review and approve past minutes
Director's Report
Treasurer's Report
Member Survey
Planning for Board Retreat—Topics: Fundraising, Programming, finance, vision, Membership, Long-term and short-term goals, Improvements, etc.
Upcoming events—Super Saturday, Valentine's Day, Bake Sale, Spring Fling
Projects: Art room, Computer Lab
Membership Directors
Other Matters

After approving past minutes, the Director gave her report. Within this report, she initiated talk about other topics on the agenda, such as the "art room," even though it is listed under projects near the end of the agenda. Once the new topic was introduced, members began to talk about that topic. Contributions included references to personal experiences related to the topic.[61] As far as I could tell, none of the members were asked to research or prepare to discuss any topics at this meeting. Yet, members are aware that a topic listed on the current agenda has been carried over from a previous meeting. For instance, in the minutes from the meeting prior to this one, under the subtitle, "Art Room Update" it states, "Need an estimate for a simple cabinet with a top to the left of the sink as a food area." At the end of the paragraph, one board member, AM, "mentioned that her nephew is a cabinet-maker and may help for low price." Given the history of this topic, during this February meeting the topic of art room is considered relevant. The Chair changes to a different topic only after lengthy discussion has ensued.

```
106.   (3.0)
107.   LB:      O.k. Different topic. We mailed um our taxes on time. Before January
108.            15 because our fiscal year ends at the end of August and I got it in before that.
109.            Um, in the library we have new computers in there, if you haven't had a chance
110.            to walk in there before the night's over, before you go, take a peek in, it looks
111.            nice. The shelves have been installed for the computers. And um, the person
112.            who installed the shelves, we asked him to take a look at the art room, we've
113.            been talking to him about the fact that we wanted to put some sort of storage in
114.            the art room, between the table and the wall. And if he could do something that
115.            is the same height as the sink so it could have some storage somehow above it
116.            and some storage below it. So we could put the microwave and toaster oven in
117.            the same spot all on the other side of the room, so we could clear up the other
118.            side of the room. And he suggested we put sliding doors on the bottom because
119.            it would take up less floor space, open it (( )) so everyone doesn't trip over
120.            the doors, which I thought was a good idea. So he designed something very
121.            simple with sliding doors and a top because it would take up less space. And
122.            then we were talking about a top that would be durable so we were talking about
123.            different materials, Formica, Corian and marble. And he actually said, marble
124.            was least expensive with a marble top, sliding doors. But, he was also going to
125.            check slate, the price of slate so he was going to call me back. With a marble
126.            top, sliding doors, birch wood, it would be, uh (.), 2,300 for storage unit and he
127.            would build part of it at home and install it here. So he did a beautiful job in the
128.            computer room. So whenever we're ready to do this if we can ((clears throat)), I
129.            can recommend him
```

At the outset of this long speaking turn (107–129), the Director declared that she was introducing a new topic (line 107) and then quickly changed the topic from filing taxes to a shelving project that had been completed. This was a segueway into the topic that dominated the discussion for the next several minutes: proposing building a shelf in the art room. During the presentation of this proposal, the Director describes the details of the shelf. When the Director concludes her monologue with a recommendation of the same person who built the computer room shelf (line 129), a new turn is taken. The Co-President uses her turn to direct attention to the person being considered to engage in the project, rather than the plan itself. In this way, the Co-President effectively manages to focus the group's on this topic, even though it was initiated during the Director's report and not listed on the agenda as the next item.

130. JS: What is his name?
131. LB: Loni Smith, he does cabinets, he's very nice and I have his fliers in
132. different places, so when everyone's ready, I can give him a call. He's been very
133. neat, punctual, which I love and very nice to work with.

A focus on the name of the person leads to a reiteration of his attributes; he is "neat, punctual" and "very nice" (line 133). The Director speaks in a way that seems to presume that the idea of this man building the cabinets is a foregone conclusion. "When everyone's ready" (line 132) and "whenever we're ready to do this" (line 128). The Director also uses "we" repeatedly (beginning in lines 111–113), to suggest that others were in on the plan (even though it seems that she's introducing it now). After establishing who is being considered to do the work, the work itself is discussed by all of the members.

134. JS: what's the space again?
135. KRM: it's between the sink and the (( ))
136. JS: where we have the table now
137. KRM: there's all those crates and things so it'd be nice clean space and
138. everything would be stored underneath it
139. JS: and nothing, that price is just for underneath like behind ((hand gesture))
140. cabinets underneath
141. LB: then he would build something along the microwave
142. KC: (( ))
143. KRM: He was trying to build a little table thing that could be on top of
144. the cabinet
144. cause then you could put the, um, the broiler and microwave on top, so they'd be
145. near an outlet, so when the children come
146. LB: and also we need it, so he wouldn't have to drill holes in the tile that was the
147. reason he started suggesting that, he'd just.
148. KRM: Right, right, yea you don't want to go
149. LB: What I like about him, he helps you figure out, he does problem solving.
150. He does a nice job.
151. JS: Does he have a sketch?
152. LB: he doesn't

153. JS: sounds good, price doesn't sound too bad
154. KC: it's not something that could be drilled into the wall
155. LC: it would be free-standing
156. KRM: you could always take it with you if you lost the space
157. TM: last time Carol from Kwainis was going to have someone come and give
158. a competing bid?
159. LB: her broth, her husband did come and he did give a competing bid. It was
160. a little bit lower, it wasn't much lower and then I just felt I had more confidence,
161. his guys were like construction people and they would've just done it on the side.
162. I'd rather have a furniture-maker heh heh do it than a construction-maker. I
163. mean they knew about plywood and stuff. I just felt that aesthetically, I'd rather
164. have a cabinet-maker than a builder. I know him.
165. JS:
166. LB: yea, yea, I'm sure the other would be fine, knew Loni longer.
167. JS: do you think. There's just a couple things we need to find out and then
168. we could vote on next board meeting, I tell you what comes to mind with me,
169. marble could crack.
170. AF: slate could do same thing, Corian is stronger.
171. What is full use of the thing?
172. AF: Even the birch, how are they going to treat the birch?
173. How finish? Birch?
174. KS: Probably polyurethane
175. Why not just have a wood top?
176. AF: what about the top they put in science labs?
177. LB: it's slate
178. AF: That's slate, you have to coat it with something
179. slate is indestructible and within twenty-four hours you wipe it off
180. JS: What about Formica?
181. LB: Formica he said was actually more expensive than marble. My experience
182. with Formica it's flamable. My parent's had a big fire in their house
183. JS: maybe we could find out the Corian versus marble
184. AF: small space
185. JS: Corian is nice
186. KRM: said need big piece
187. KC: stains, crack
188. KRM: marble has that shiny finish on it, that's not going to stain at all though
189. scrub it off
190. KRM: do they treat top of it or just the stone?
191. just shine it up
192. AF: Is there a difference between marble and granite?
193. JS: would someone want to, would you find different prices?
194. Do you want to find out?
195. LB: I was going to try to. The H & W foundation had given us money
196. for the computer room so I didn't ask for any money this year. I don't know if
197. they give 3 years in a row, so I thought I would ask them to help us with the
198. art room today. Try to take a picture of computer room, it's so little. So I just

199. showed them how we spent the money.
200. I'd like to just see. We can still do all the voting but I just thought?
201. JS: It's nice to have it together by fall, so all right so we'll just kind of leave that
202. open until next meeting and you can bring that sketch
203. LB: And, K(RM) has been working together on nice designs for the walls,

In this fairly mundane example of the need to select a countertop surface and contract a builder for the work, the members of this board of directors raise points related to the way the decision will be made and co-determine, through this talk, what is relevant to discuss when making decisions here. By breaking this segment into three sections, I hoped to call attention to some salient features: topic introduction (lines 109–127), Question/Answer about specifics (lines 130–133), and challenges or alternate suggestions to the proposal (lines 134–203).

Initially, this segment began during the Director's report (from lines 109–127). By introducing this topic when she had the floor, the Director was able to propose a nearly complete plan including: a need for the project, a design, and a person to complete the work. When reviewing the presentation of the plan, it seems that the Director crafted it in such a way as to gain agreement. When the floor changed after the Director's presentation, it was the Co-President who moved the conversation in the direction of a decision ("do all the voting"). Then, board members raised questions about the design of the shelf specifically, not about the need for the project, nor about the person being contracted (with one exception). Finally, the topic concluded by being shifted to another project being undertaken.

One device the Director used to include all the board members in the decision is by referring to everyone involved as "we." Although we could consider the influence of leadership as a primary factor in cases of group decision-making,[62] how this influence is interactionally accomplished is more significant. For instance, rather than stating her own opinion (such as "I think"), the Director used "we" to include others in the plan (initially "the staff"). As the interaction proceeds, "we" includes the board members, as in when "we decide"—then "I can recommend him" (lines 128–129). Therefore, the decision is acknowledged to be a joint decision. After this decision-making episode, it can be acknowledged to others that board members make decisions and the Director gets the work done by carrying out those decisions on behalf of the board.

Once the topic is introduced the Co-President provides a way for board members to contribute to the discussion by asking a question about the building materials being suggested. That the builder suggested a material and a price for the materials was not questioned. In this forum, many board members chime in with questions about the "space," installation, and make suggestions about building materials and their properties for use in a countertop situation where children would be playing. Member knowledge, and/or expertise, is not called into question but presumed during this discussion (Sharrock, 1974).

When board members begin questioning the details of what is being proposed, they mainly seem to seek clarification about "what's the work?" The idea of competitive bids is raised briefly (line 115) and responded to with an acknowledgment that it was discussed (after the previous meeting) but not followed through. That this is not an issue for discussion was very curious to me, but as demonstrated by the time spent on the work itself in subsequent talk, members do not deem this issue to be relevant to their discussion.

Rather than the need for the work itself, what seemed to be most relevant were the characteristics of the person who is being considered to complete the work. For instance, the Director provided numerous justifications, such as "he did a beautiful job in the computer room" (lines 127–128), "he's been very neat, punctual" and "very nice to work with" (lines 132–133), "he helps you figure [things] out," "he does problem solving" (line 149), and "he does a nice job" (line 150). When the idea of competing bids is raised a second time, the Director offers her preference for a "furniture-maker rather than a construction-maker" and then upgrades it to, "I'd rather have a cabinet-maker than a builder" (lines 162–164). All of these statements are offered as legitimate reasons for going forward with this project.

Valid Premises for Making Decisions

As Tompkins and Cheney (1985) have argued, groups often use particular premises—both value and factual—for making decisions. In many discussions at the Family Center, participants include in their descriptions of persons and things a comment about how pleasant they are. During these discussions, a description of something or someone as "nice" functions as part of a legitimate reason, or decisional premise, for hiring the person to work at the Center. Consider the following:

141.   It's *nice* to have it together by fall, so all right, leave that open until next meeting
142.   And, K ((RM)) has been working together on *nice* designs for the walls,

174.   LB: Formica comes in *nice* colors.
175.   KC: so, what's the objection to marble? ((everyone glances in her direction))
176.   Marble does stain.

286.   JS: Well let's keep it with that date.
287.   If you wanted to, it might be *nice*.
288.   LB: We could do it at my house, sure
289.   She's volunteering, two kids
290.   (pause)
291.   LB: thought it was *nice*, Carol was helping here

Maintaining Membership Through Meetings 47

292. JS: when is she going to do the cooking?

385. G does a class
386. KRM: she does a brilliant class. It's really *nice*, she just has this whole way she does it, she does all this stretching and (um hmm) ballet, she'll sometimes use French words, she actually getting them to think about how to use their bodies
387. she should do it here
388. LB: she is

In these segments, an evaluative statement, such as "she does a brilliant class" (line 386; or "it might be nice," line 287) are used to justify decisions about hiring someone to teach a class or to complete work by a certain date. These types of evaluations are significant for determining the goodness of fit for accomplishing tasks at the Family Center. When a participant interjects, "she does such a nice job," the candidate for the position is considered a strong candidate. Other claims or justifications that might be typical for other organizations, such as credentials, degrees, and professional associations are absent. Personal references or previous contact with someone from the Center, including such statements as, "I was at a workshop" (line 505), are used to create legitimacy for action. When no one has had any personal experience with a potential hire, then that person has not been hired, such as the dance group referred to below (line 515).

512. M1:[63] he was good
513. M2: I've never seen him
514. AM: I was thinking of him for Reesa's birthday, he was very good
515. M3: So we don't want the dance group
516. M4: Can we see a video?

In this segment (lines 512–516), one of the board members (AM) makes an evaluative statement, "he was good" as a reply to another board member who had "never seen him." If making certain that there is a personal connection or history with a potential participant, then the claim "I've never seen him" (513) is met with a specific personal reference related to using this person's services for her own child's birthday party to substantiate the earlier claim "he was good" (line 512). The next person asks about "the dance group" using the pronoun "we" to indicate that a group decision seems to have been made because talk has proceeded away from continuing to consider a former performer option (for the Spring Fling). The next person picks up on the suggestion of reconsidering the dance group by asking to see the video. Therefore, the contrast between the dance group who does not have a personal reference with the person who was at the birthday party (a magician) demonstrates the acceptable way of introducing and deciding on particular performers for this upcoming Center event. The performers with the personal reference are decided on favorably and those without are considered for the following year, or otherwise not able to be decided on for this year because there is no person to vouch for this group's "goodness."

As the instances just noted illustrate, members rely on familiarity with a service provider when making decisions about who to hire. On the basis of these examples, nonparticipants might look at these transcripts or watch the video and audio tapes and believe that if members think someone is "good," or "nice" that is an adequate reason for engaging in their services. What about "expenses?" Although the cost of some services is brought up and discussed,[64] it does not have the same legitimacy or weight in decision making at this Center. Another example may provide more clarification.

During this same February 2001 meeting, the Director brought up hiring an exterminator for consideration by the board after being solicited on the telephone by a service provider. At no prior meeting had there been talk about an "insect problem." Therefore, in presenting the issue, the Director had to legitimize a course of action which included,

1. a presentation of the problem as an uncontestable (legitimate) problem;
2. a description about kinds of insects: ants, flying ants, and so on (including others in this discussion)
3. the use of this provider as opposed to others (this is achieved conversationally by appealing to an unstated rule, that the procedure does not "harm children") and evidence that this provider does not charge higher and higher fees (as others have been known to do);
4. therefore go with this vendor (ask board to approve the decision).

A discussion ensues to question the premises based on,

1. extent of the problem, because it was not previously described or known by members of the board (even those who had been there for a lengthy period of time);
2. evidence of the effectiveness of this service provider
   - Who knows someone else?
   - Who else has had this problem?
   - What are the alternate courses of action?
   - What have other members done personally when confronted with such a problem?

This subject was given a considerable amount of time during this meeting. Later during this meeting, members expressed dismay at a lack of time to have a thoughtful discussion about an agenda item that was considered more urgent (an upcoming fundraising event) that was only introduced during the last 15 minutes of the meeting after at least two members had left.

In the conversational sequence of hiring an exterminator, the President joined in defining the issue as, "we had a rat problem..." Each member who took a speaking turn did so if they had some personal experience to relate (a rodent or insect problem in their house or apartment). No member denied or contradicted the experience of another. Given this way of presenting information, by giving an opinion in the form of a personal account ("what I did was..."), makes it difficult for others to challenge any one such statement. Statements are not offered as "objective" evidence, therefore they are not able to be "objectively" denied or challenged. Rather, by using the personal form everyone gets their say.[65] The question then becomes, what can the group do with this kind of information? How is a decision, for this group, supposed to be reached? How are statements of equal weight valued or ranked so as to lead to a particular course of action?

By presenting each board member's opinion on the decision-making matter at hand, a board member is able to present her experience to add to the collective store of information. This addition of information can be characterized as a legitimate way of making decisions[66] here.

After each member adds a personal opinion or experience (if applicable), the sequence ends when one member volunteers to find the number of the exterminating service she had recommended. The President volunteers to "negotiate" with the original, soliciting service-provider and the Director says that we will "try them out for one time." So, it seems that during this instance, board members have learned about the problem and offered their experiences. They have positioned themselves as potential candidates to help solve the problem, with relevant knowledge and contacts to be of some use to the Center.

Through this way of speaking, an individual member can now carry out the task that has been made legitimate by the assembled board members. The President often formalizes this course of action by asking for an individual to commit to enacting the group's decision, "will you follow up on that?"

In the exterminator example, after the board meeting, the Director is in the position of giving an answer to the soliciting service-provider, but now, because there was a decision-making discussion held by the Board of Directors, she can refer to the larger board to give weight to her answer. The Director even states this baldly as, "I can just tell them the board decided..." This reinforces the Director's position as board spokesperson, rather than having to give them her personal opinion (which was one possible option she could have chosen).

What can we say of this interactional sequence? We notice that turns are taken to give legitimacy to a form of talk called "decision making." That, for this form to be enacted in groups, more than one member must offer an opinion (or statement), and that the form itself must include the decision-making parts as follows:

- problem is identified and described
- options are discussed, eliminated, weighed
- optimal choices are posed as legitimate and actionable
- persons are identified as able or willing to carry out one or more actions the group decides on.

This group conducted a form of communication known as "decision making" during a meeting scheduled for the purpose of making decisions. When the topic was introduced, the group worked together interactionally to produce this common communicative form. For organizations to function as they do, members coordinate their actions and "talk" to get things done. Meetings become the forum for a Director to legitimate her role and her external conversations by positioning such sayings as the possession of the organization. These board member discussions create a "decision outcome" because their talk can be labeled a "decision" to others. These meetings also provide opportunities for members of the board to lend their expertise when engaged in decision-making discussions about mundane matters, such as countertop surfaces and insects and to "help" the Center by assigning themselves actions outside of the meetings. The main way that this is formalized is through the action of "voting."

Outcomes of Decisions: Votes

One of the reasons that board meetings are often thought to be the place where decisions reside is presumably the "voting" that board members undertake to make any act official. This process is one that has a formal structure in parliamentary procedure and texts such as *Robert's Rules of Order* (Patnode, 1989). There are several examples of voting in the board meetings I attended. If you listen closely, voting seems to follow a lengthy discussion wherein what is said seems more likely to constitute the decision itself than the voting that concludes the discussion.

In the Family Center example just cited, first we hear the Co-President say, "we could vote on next meeting" (line 168) and then we hear the Director say "we can still do all the voting" (line 200) to indicate that a decision must be made official by a vote from the board, but that the vote will not be taken until the next meeting. In this case, the issue is going to be left "open." Because board members raised numerous questions and answers needed to be sought, par-

Maintaining Membership Through Meetings   51

ticipants withheld the vote. However, for an action to occur as a result of a vote, especially an action that might be taken during the month between meetings, a vote by the board is important for the Director to obtain. Therefore, being able to "do all the voting" is a way to get information that board members desired later, but to gain approval for the general idea of the project.

At the PRC, voting was typical. There were only a few instances where decision making was much less formal, as illustrated by the statement,

PL: I would like to leave this decision in the hands of the President (May meeting)

More frequently, the voting process was much more formalized. First, members ensured that a "quorum"[67] is reached. During the vote itself, a member made a motion, "move to a vote" and another member "seconded" the motion (see Patnote, 1989). In a series of turns, voting was collaboratively accomplished by several participants. In one case, the President of the board asks a question that is followed by another board members' addition to the question and completed with a "motion" by a third board member. In this way, three board members (HT, SH, RM) worked together to build a motion that can be "seconded" and voted on (approved) by the others in the meeting. Described by Milburn (2002) as "collaboratively built sentences,"[68] often times when members use a phrase such as "Is there a motion?" it is repeated "by the next speaker who helps to complete the sentence" (p. 295). The segment below demonstrates the full voting procedure.[69]

During the March board meeting, about midway through a discussion about the spring festival, the members jointly produced a vote by making a motion in several parts.

390. PL: let's take a vote that
391. RM: we already have a quorum
392. SH: oh, that's the missing thing that I
393.   our Cultural is meeting on there
394.   oh, . . . [Spanish words]
395. JG: read your minutes
396. SH: I didn't have no minutes
397. RM: you gotta get 'em to read 'em
398.   what are we looking for in terms of a motion,
399.   approving an offer?
400.   of paying them?
401. HT: 1 dollar per head, 'till 6 p.m.
402. RM: 'till 6 p.m.
403.   from what time?
404.   from 3 o'clock
405. JG: from the time the parade ends

406. SH: oh, that's going to be alot of people then
407. RM: could you be more precise
408. [CR, RM talking simultaneously]
409. RM: what's J gonna be out here with a starting pistol
410. JG: but, but you're gonna find that not everyone in that parade is going to go to the festival
411. So,
412. LG: some are going to go home and change
413. SH: my point is that we were going on the assumption that
414. we were going on the assumption that usually from 3 to 6,
415. *esta hora muerta,*
416. it's not going to be this year
417. JG: no,
418. which is good for us,
419. SH: oh, it's wonderful
420. LG: and that was their feeling,
421. that they're generating our bulk
422. SH: o.k.
423. LG: but they wanted a piece of it
424. JG: but they wanted it the entire Sunday
425. and I said no,
426. after the parade is over, you really don't
427. generate people
428. RM: they do have substantial expenses, including
429. they have the permits, right?
430. what do they cost?
431. PS: for the parade I'm not sure
432. LG: what about for the park?
433. PS: we're working with that now, to transfer that
434. TM: they paid a $200 deposit
435. PS: $200 deposit
436. RM: plus $2,000 for the cops and I don't know what else.
437. I'll move to question.
438. LG: who are you moving it to?
439. SH: you move to what?
440. RM: I'll move to make the offer to PRHA
441. LG: I'll second
442. SH: He hasn't said the whole motion,
443. go ahead
444. EC: Motion to accept the proposal [RM: yes, thank you] by the PRHA [RM: exactly],
445. uh, one dollar until 6 p.m.on the 23rd.
446. LG: 3 to 6 p.m.
447. EC: 3 to 6 p.m.
448. SH: why couldn't he make the motion?
449. why are you . . .

```
450.  RM:   that's the motion
451.  SH:   then I'll second that
452.  HT:   all in favor?
453.        aye
454.  LG:   opposed? [hammers table]
```

When a formal decision needs to be made, a member will indicate that a "vote" needs to be taken (line 390). In order to vote, quorum needs to be met (see line 391). Then, a formal motion that specifies all of the details needs to be clearly stated. In this segment, we see that the motion itself is jointly constructed between several members (lines 398, 437, 438, 439, 440, 442, 444, 448, and 450). When a motion is made, members continue adding information in order to help complete the act. Finally, the motion is "seconded" (line 451) and voted on by "aye" (line 453). The repetitions, turn overlap, and joint constructions of the motion demonstrate the group accomplishment of a formal vote. One could argue that calling for a vote signals the intention that the group be jointly responsible for what occurs within the organization (rather than a single individual, such as the Director), and that in the process of "doing all the voting" the group symbolizes its joint accomplishment of making a decision.

In contrast to Tompkins and Cheney (1985), where management exercise "control" or influence over employees by getting them to accept organizational premises, I have tried to demonstrate that personal premises become organizational premises when enacted in actual conversations. That is, the organizational premises do not pre-exist. Members themselves, by participating in organizational conversations, construct or formulate what comes to be known as "decisions" and "decision-making" talk. This talk includes valued and therefore, valid, decisional premises that justify future actions. In the meetings themselves, the participants create a social structure by enacting rules such as quorum, making motions and voting, to formalize their talk into decisions for which future action is held accountable.

Discussion

According to traditional decision-making theories, actors prune away less viable options and the decision is the route that is left. An examination of accounts for how circumstances come to be, helps us to recognize the work that interactants do with one another to construct particular worlds, or organizations within which decisions appear to be made and through which they are made sensible (Weick, 1979, 1995[70]). As shown in the instances just noted, the discourse process commonly known as the communicative form, "decision making," is not entirely retrospective (as Weick, 1995 has postulated[71]) and as not entirely based on accounts (also as Weick, 1995 has postulated), but as sequentially accomplished by members. When one member volunteers to do some kind of work ("following up"), then an in-meeting decision meets external-meeting action. After following a vote, any action that was based on the group's decision can be reported back to the group at a subsequent meeting.

Decisions are not as neatly constructed as some management researchers have suggested. Based on the analysis of several instances of board meeting discussion, deliberation, and voting, one can note that institutional members co-construct agreed-on rationale in order to conclude that a satisfactory decision has been made. Even though some literature focuses on how individuals supply various candidate arguments, I have tried to emphasize the collaborative work of the entire board when encountering an instance for which a "decision" is called. In this way, all of the members work together to create what can be documented as having been decided.

At times, the process of making a decision arises *before* subsequent action takes place (or can take place legitimately). This presumption of future action often entails an accounting before the action in order to justify why a given course should proceed or not. Members make claims, and in the process, use premises, to legitimize a course of action that becomes sensible to the group. When the group engages in such talk, then members help to co-construct the entire process: what counts as the decision, the problem, a solution or solutions, and who may enact the decision. In these ways, participants "formulate" and "reformulate" claims—what talk is decision talk? what counts as a decision (that may be recorded in minutes)? how a decision should be marked (by a vote)? and how past formulations (we decided that . . .) create a place for present action? By formulating some talk as "decision making," members both reify previous norms and create new norms for what "should" happen in the future.

Within all of the decision talk, what is usual or normal behavior for any group becomes part of the basis for its claims about membership. That is, the boundaries of members are, at least partially determined by what the group deems normal or ordinary behavior. "How people behave tells us what is the right way to behave" (Pomerantz, 1986, p. 228). Pomerantz (1986) claims that some formulations actually diffuse responsibility from an individual. However, one could also claim that in speaking this way, individual group members build "social accountability" and will act in ways that they have negotiated are legitimate ways to act based on organization decisions.

Within this chapter, then, we have a specific way of defining and examining member decisions. First, a decision occurs within an event. For EC scholars, this is a speech act within a communicative event (Schwartzman, 1989). In order to create the speech act of decisions, members formulate some talk within a meeting as talk that warrants a "decision" or an issue that needs a "vote" (Pomerantz, 1986; Schegloff, 1972a). Once some talk is formulated (or reformulated) as "decision" talk, then participants use "premises" (Tompkins & Cheney, 1985) to discuss, debate and legitimize future actions. These actions conclude in a formal "vote" or a decision that has been made and can serve to "normalize" behavior or create the norms within which the group operates.

Summary

By virtue of occurring within a nonprofit organization, board meeting talk is presumed to be sanctioned talk. It is talk that fits within a broad notion of what it means to be an organization, an organizational participant, and a nonprofit business in the United States. Nonprofit organizational interaction follows a recognizable sequence and conforms to what we consider recognizable work. When analyzing board meeting practices, and noticing dialogue that is about mundane issues, some may take these very practices as the ones that demonstrate how inefficient and ineffective nonprofit organizations are and criticize them for not being "business-like" enough (Drucker, 2001). However, if one takes the instances in their own right, rather than comparing an idealized, for-profit business discussion with what really does occur in many meetings (both for-profit and nonprofit) where topics are discussed until they are sufficiently resolved to the satisfaction of those participants present at the given meeting; then we can begin to understand how important it is to examine in a very nuanced way, the actual meeting talk that is part of any decision, be it small or large.

In this chapter, I have tried to demonstrate how members' talk during meetings helps to constitute a sense of membership itself. Decisions are made by members who know how to speak in a way that is reasonable to other members. What makes any speaker provide "valid" reasons for action is, at least partially, dependent upon that individual members' knowledge of valid member categories—that is, categories for actions. As Baker (1997) has noted, people talk in terms of types or "categories" and these are then linked to rules for behavior that create "category-bound activities."

What is also category bound is talk as "decision making." This formulation is a category of talk that, when produced, creates board members as "decision makers" whose work influences each nonprofit center's operations.

Within these microinstances, participants create meaning in two ways. First, as agents we have choices in how we speak. Those choices are made evident in our utterances. Fortunately, I have been able to record the utterances of Center members to be able to document the conversational choices made. Second, meaning can be considered an interactional accomplishment that unfolds through the progress of conversations.

Although Deetz and Simpson (2004) assert that, "the ability to make mutually satisfactory decisions together may well be a stronger basis for community than mutual understanding" (p. 151), those decisions can only be made mutually satisfying when members are able to coordinate their actions through some common knowledge of how to do things in each nonprofit center. However, when circumstances change, sometimes those decisional premises for action become either more entrenched or may be purposefully altered to suite the participants and the organization.

Chapter 4

Organizational Change

Organizational change literature (Bridges, 1991; Hamel & Prahalad, 1996; Kanter, Stein & Jick, 1992; Kotter, 1996; Mintzberg, 1994; Schein, 1973; Tichy, 1983) is replete with references to "change"—the need to change, preparing and planning for change, and implementing new change processes. In this literature, the premise is that stability is the norm, and change is a new, sometimes unexpected occurrence. If one begins with a communication perspective, as taken in this volume, one will recognize that change is a common everyday occurrence and that stability is actually only a momentary snapshot.

Organizational change initiatives often include the assumptions that change is the term for the global or organization-wide differences that are brought about because of a precipitous event—merger, acquisition, downsizing, reengineering, or strategic planning. This kind of change involves the entire organization. Often senior organizational members decide that "things should be different around here." How these differences are brought about often takes place in many meetings.[72] What these meetings have in common is an explicit focus on "the way we do things around here." One might even be so bold as to suggest that it's like a meta-ethnomethodology: We know that we do things and we know we have made sense of them in a certain way, now let us reflect on that and see what we can do differently.

This focus on "the way we do things around here," may include an examination of "processes," "forms," and "structures." Depending on how "large" the change initiative is (size is a common metaphor), the change could include an entire re-examination of job titles and reporting lines.[73] The change that occurs, thus, includes assumptions about what counts as change (its definitions) and what processes or work is subject to examination and revision.

Undergoing change, then, includes presumptions about what counts as communication. However, the organization's focus is not necessarily on how participants communicate, but rather, how members do their jobs. Whether participants explicitly focus on the process of communication, one can recognize that they enact or assume that an organization is a continuous achievement that is sustained by ongoing conversations, documents, and reifying processes.

Members, like the organizations to which they belong, use referencing and other communicative devices to historicize their group or organization. By using common references (indexing), members talk themselves into a stable system. In the process of interacting, members and organizations constantly change. However, not all change is planned nor predictable. Purposeful change can be contrasted with the unanticipated departure of a board member. Termination or voluntary separation from an organization offers a glimpse into the patterned ways of accounting for actions that are valued as opposed to a discourse that is offered that begins to differentiate the departing member.[74]

Due to the growth of strategic planning as a way to optimize the effectiveness of organizations (Mintzberg, 1994; Porter, 1979, 1980, 1987, 1996), many nonprofit boards began re-examining the work that they do by engaging their board in strategic planning meetings. Peter Drucker (2001) has advised nonprofit managers to adopt efficient business practices and to engage in strategic planning in order to focus their fundraising efforts, or before embarking on a major capital campaign. During my participation at both centers, they each embarked on a formal strategic planning process.

Often, one of the first steps in strategic planning is an off-site meeting.[75] Both the Puerto Rican Center and the Family Center held strategic planning retreats that I was able to record. Both retreats were held off-site. The PRC retreat was broken into two sessions, at two different locations. The Family Center retreat was limited to a 1-day event. I was not involved in planning the PRC event, but was integrally involved in planning the Family Center retreat.

When a discussion arose during one of the FC monthly meetings about the "annual retreat," I introduced the notion of having the retreat facilitated by someone outside of the Center's staff and board. Having attended the PRC retreat that was facilitated by a third party (who was suggested by one of the other board members), I thought that the group dynamics changed due to the presence of an outsider who helped to direct our conversations in new ways. Therefore, I recommended a facilitator to the FC President.[76] She agreed to meet with the facilitator and to accept his offer to facilitate the retreat pro bono.

In this chapter, I first demonstrate how organizational members talk about change by citing several examples from each center's strategic planning retreat. Following these examples, I describe an example of a board member who came to the PRC board to terminate her membership. In both of these instances of change, members express key organizational values and commitments.

Strategic Change

The aims of any strategic planning process include examining the organizational mission and creating a vision to achieve new goals or directions. The FC planning session was purposefully created to accomplish "idea-sharing, visioning, setting goals, and the need to get away from routine." The facilitator, who was contracted to help the group with strategic planning, prompted the President, JS, to articulate these at an exploratory meeting that was held prior to the actual retreat meeting. From these goals, then, the facilitator suggested that the group (a) "create a statement that identifies the purpose of the Center"; (b) collect and review any data the group might find useful pertaining to four previously defined areas of improvement for the Center (membership, programs, fundraising, and physical improvements); and (c) try to identify goals that could be achieved in the upcoming year after the retreat. The facilitator designed these suggestions to create an opportunity for the Co-President to shift the focus of the retreat from setting goals to creating action plans.

Retreat[77]

The retreat meeting was held in the home of the Center's Director (LB), which is in the same neighborhood as the Center. The living room served as the meeting space, with additional chairs placed around the perimeter of the room to form a circle. The décor clearly marked the space as a home, and the Director played the dual roles of host and meeting participant (e.g., repeatedly getting up to answer the phone and the doorbell). This setting mirrored the familiar setting of the monthly board meetings in that, although it was away from the Center, the interruptions and casual seating arrangement in a room used for other purposes remained. In both meetings, members arrived and left as necessary. The main differences between the strategic planning retreat and the monthly board meetings were the addition of a facilitator, the morning meeting time and length,[78] and the fact that food was served.

There were 11 participants in the Family Center board retreat; nine women and two men. Kenefick, one of the two males, was introduced as the facilitator; the other male participant, MF, Co-President along with JS, arrived about halfway through the meeting. Kenefick clarified his role at the retreat as an "observer" who watches the process in order not to intervene in what he called the "content," but in order to keep time, take notes, and make observations. Throughout the ensuing discussions, Kenefick used the agenda that had been created prior to the retreat (as well as affirmed at the outset of the meeting) as a device to help the group members focus and reflect on their use of time in talking about any one topic.

The agenda included the following topics: competition from other centers in the neighborhood, fundraising, programs to offer, and physical improvements to the Center. These topics demonstrate which areas of the Center are important, and because they are listed on an agenda for a strategic-planning meeting, they also indicate the areas that have been targeted for change. For example, with respect to programs, the group debated the possibility of including music classes and offering a full range of programs that could position the Center as a reasonable substitute for preschool. Never was the idea of doing away with programs suggested—merely a new composition of the class offerings was suggested. This demonstrates the way that one area can be seen as essential to the concept of the Center,[79] whereas another can be modified without damaging the organization itself.

The physical setting was one area where ideas ranged from getting a new space, to simply improving the condition of the current space. KS, for example, stated that she was interested in improving the physical environment of the organization: "My main interest is helping with the physical improvements, making it a place where kids and parents like to come, so making it more appealing especially the art room." It was decided that the space could be better used and that artwork and murals could make it look more attractive. The group also agreed to put up appropriate instructional signs at strategic places in the Center.

During this retreat, members engaged in a lengthy discussion about the individual needs of board members and their children. During the discussion, individual members, and their responsibilities for activities scheduled by the Center, became implicated. For instance, AF stated her goal of having the Center "focus on the 3–5-age group," and LB responded by saying:

555. We did try science, but not for that . . . we can always start again. We stopped
556. it because we didn't have enough kids to sign up for science. We tried a nature (.)
557. with me and Jennifer ((laughs)) and that was it. We tried (.) but we didn't get
558. anybody, so we keep trying things and then we don't have enough people.

In these lines, the participants involved expressed an orientation to taking of personal responsibility within the Center. As the Director of the Center, LB schedules classes. The board members have children and claim to "want" to take classes that, unfortunately, did not suit their family's schedules. The Director described her actions as "trying" to accommodate these needs, but failing to do so due to a lack of enrollment. Therefore, she put the onus back onto the interested board members, by suggesting that another member (AF), or others in general, get several people together to form a class. This shift from the personal responsibility of the Director, the one paid to run the Center, to those making the criticism (or request)—a parent, board member, or the other Center members—demonstrates the active role everyone should play in the organizing and running of the Center.

Although certain norms for behavior, such as "everyone should play a role in organizing" as mentioned earlier are evident in the interactions during this retreat, another kind of talk was also present that called this norm into question. At times, certain members seemed to speak as if it was more important to maintain the Center in its status quo rather than engage in a change. Such phrases such as "we tried that" were made by both the Director and the male Co-President, both of whom had longer tenure with the organization than the other board members and seemed to discourage suggestions for change made by other members.

For instance, when retreat participants began to mention ideas for raising funds for the Center, the Co-President, MF responded to one idea with a direct "no" indicating disagreement. Other negative responses, such as "well, we cannot do that again" served to signal rejection and a negative evaluation of some members' ideas and changed the rhythm of the talk that had been established at this retreat meeting. After the lunch break, MF dominated the discussion. He continually answered when a question was asked by another participant and evaluated any suggestion made. This type of speaking style was unique to this participant and was quite different from the style of JS, the other Co-President.

These responses may indicate the desire for continuity amidst the pull for change. They also demonstrate a tension between newer board members and older members—who rely on historical knowledge of how things were and how they came to be the way they are now to justify *not* adopting the new suggestions or making changes.

Not only is change the topic of conversation, but it also characterizes the interactional tone. During the first 90 minutes, members' voices were medium-pitched and nonconfrontational. If a participant did not agree with a suggestion made by another, it was not stated overtly but in a manner such as, "What about . . .?" Later, when MF joined the meeting, changes were immediately evident in the tone of the meeting. MF, in contrast, rejected ideas outright by making remarks, such as "I don't see it" or "I don't think there's an avenue to do that." The dynamics of the group interaction also changed because his turns of talk were both more frequent and lengthier than other members' turns.

The following example was preceded by a discussion about the physical space of the Center and the limitations of owning a building in the neighborhood where the Center is located:

1250. MF: I don't know how many billions of dollars they raised and they bought a
1251. brownstone . . .
1260. MF: You have to have a plan how much square footage we really need . . .
1261. AF: mmm hmm
1265. MF: Yes, that's all possible I'd say (1.0)
1266. JK: Well, it's up to this group to decide, what you want to do
1267.   and what you want to do over the next year
1268. MF: That's right
1269. JK: So, that's what this day is for, right.

In this instance, Kenefick (JK) redirected the focus of the comment made by MF from his ability to decide and pronounce what was possible for the group in his role as Co-President (line 1265) to the work of "the group" members in the room to make a "decision" together ("it's up to this group to decide," line 1266).

Another example of maintaining the status quo was made by the male Co-President

1520. JK: OK, reactions from the group?
1521. MF: I'll give you some feedback from the nannies, since they're not here. First of
1522. all, the idea of doing the pillows on the floor, not going to be going for that at all
1523. We wanted to put new chairs in and the first thing they said was there are no arms
1524. on the chairs. So, the idea of sitting on the floor, that's not going to fly. It's a good
1525. idea to try get ideas, . . . I did informal surveys, . . . so I think it's a good idea to
1526. solicit information because they do have good ideas. . . . It might be great to try.
1527. JK: Other reactions? Or where you might be able to see a role for yourself in what
1528. this group was talking about
1529. (4.0) OK, last group
1530. JS: Well, we tried . . .

Although one interpretation of this segment is that prior to the arrival of MF, the group had established a precedent of expressing suggestions openly (see Milburn, Kenefick, & Lambert, 2005); however, it can also be the case that the statement exhibits a resistance to change.

When organizational changes occur, they may be planned or unplanned. However, in the case of strategic planning, part of the process demands for participants to be "reflexively" aware of their role in constructing "change." This process involves speaking, taking responsibility for suggestions and making commitment to actions that will affect change.

Often times, a member (as in the case of the Co-President) may openly resist a suggestion for change by appealing to what was already tried in the past. These conversations demonstrate sticking points for those members who would like things to be different and for those who are not willing to revise or take steps to make those differences happen.

Long-Term Planning

At the PRC, we participated in what was termed "long-term planning." Some referenced the event as a "retreat" for the "5-year plan."

119. JG: And PL and I helped work on that restructuring,
120. the the 5-year plan for the agency.
121. We don't have a 5-year plan for the agency
122. We, I'm hoping that when we go away on the *retreat*
123. and before these people come to monitor us

124. which will be sometime in January, mid, the latter part of January
125. that at least we can have something for them. (December board meeting)

In this segment, the plan is not positioned as a change for the agency, rather, it is an object that will be produced for "people" (line 123), who will be "monitoring us" (presumably a granting or funding agency).

The PRC strategic planning began by the President of the board describing the objective as working on "short- and long-term goals." He introduced the facilitator who clarified the plans for the day as work on the "strategic plan" by referring to the mission statement of the Center and a previous version of a strategic plan that was begun more than a year before this meeting (as clarified by the Director). The facilitator described her role as creating a "structure" for completing the plan, to create 3–5-year goals, benchmarks, mind mapping to look at trends, looking 10 years into the future and next steps. She asked the assembled participants if this agenda sounded "OK" and everyone agreed.

The facilitator asked us to make introductions that included our names, our work with the Center, favorite place, favorite food or hobby and goals for the day. Many board members mentioned Puerto Rico as a favorite place and used the Spanish name for their favorite food. There was much good-natured banter and laughter during this segment and throughout the day.

Then the vision statement was read aloud by two different board members so that we could all hear it:

> *"The vision for the PRC is to enhance pride and self esteem within the Puerto Rican and other Spanish speaking communities by promoting, maintaining, and sharing our rich cultural heritage to promote community involvement, and foster leadership development, to meet a diverse social and economic needs of our growing community, by providing comprehensive services and to act as an advocate in shaping and influencing the issues that effect our people."*

After this another board member read the PRC mission statement while we read it on our handouts. Then we were asked to break into groups of two and three people to review the strategic plan outline (that had been drafted the prior year before this board began). Each group reported back on one of these four sections:

- finance
- youth development
- funding
- collaborating-networking

Our next task was to "share symbols." The facilitator described the task like this,

One of the things, um (.) you actually sort of go beyond looking at the Center as we know it, but think of a symbol that would reflect what you're trying to do at the PRC (.)

So, we each came up with a symbol and at times the facilitator would draw it or write it on a flip chart. The symbols included: a lighthouse, a rainbow, a dollar sign, a cornerstone of a solid foundation, a cave with sunlight at the end, a rooster showing pride, an elevator, and an umbrella. Sometimes an explanation accompanied the symbol and sometimes members joked about the symbols or drawings.

Next there was a brainstorm of trends affecting the Center and lines were drawn connecting those that were related. Finally, we had to put four dots on the trends that were most significant factors influencing the Center. Then each group took one of the four sheets of newsprint and worked with those trends for the rest of the day. This concluded day one of the strategic planning retreat.

The outcome of both planning retreats was a set of plans that were written down. These plans could be pointed to later as our goals and values. Perhaps equally significant were the ways that the facilitated conversations themselves helped to bring members together around the shared goals. By articulating individual visions for each Center, members learned what they had in common and could build on the commonalities. Similarly, when resistance to ideas surfaced, members learned the boundaries of certain actions; recognizing that some ideas would not work with certain participants.

Terminating Membership/Ceasing to Participate

A second sense of change can occur as members enter or leave the organization. Particularly when members depart, there may be an interactional moment that captures the sentiment of what it means to be a member and what it means to depart from that role.

Terminating Membership

Part of the work that members must do is to describe their actions as sensible to other members of the organization. By accounting for actions in ways that make sense to others, the group itself reifies the organizational norms and values. Organizational conversations are significant because they illustrate how membership is done in action. Furthermore, any conversation implicates moral behavior in that the members must give "reasoned" accounts of their actions. Particularly

Organizational Change 65

within organizations, the matter of giving and receiving accounts (Buttny, 1993; Scott & Lyman, 1967) is a continuous process that constructs the flow of what it means to be an organization, and an organizational member.

Interestingly, if one desires to remain an organizational participant, when a breach has occurred, one must account for one's actions by making reference to the normative framework used by other members. However, when a participant leaves an organization, or takes a different position with regard to that organization (e.g. steps down from a leadership role), membership values can be demonstrated. It is at such moments that a process of differentiation may occur.

In the following analysis, a woman who had been elected as part of the slate of board members gives an account for her absence from board meetings and, in the process, appeals to what it means to be a reasonable and good member of the community (even when clearly not fulfilling her board member duties). By focusing on this one account, it becomes very clear how the process of differentiation includes a simultaneous justification for maintaining a certain type of relationship with other members. The context for this account is part of a stream of conversation that was related to the matter of the recent board selection and election.

In the following account, Teresita has requested a meeting with the board in order to explain her actions of not attending meetings following the election. Interestingly, this account also includes a historical narrative about how the present board came to be composed. Therefore, the story is not only about the departing member, but also about how the current board members achieved their positions.

It is important to note that the actions of the account-giver were characterized as a "misunderstanding" and therefore the agency of the person is described, and hopefully perceived, as not responsible for the act as it was (mis)characterized. In this way, the account-giver justifies her actions. This justification includes the work of positioning herself as a particular kind of person (nonmember) in relation to the others (members).

Finally, by focusing on one specific account, what counts as a problem or potential problem behavior for the members is made clearer. People do not account when there is not a problem (or perceived problem). The act of account-giving makes the account-recipient, even if previously unaware, recognize that the account-giver believed there was a problem that should be addressed and rectified (also see Buttny, 2004).

First, this section of the meeting is characterized as "discussion" because the requisite number of board members to make a meeting official by having quorum has not been met.[80]

JG: o.k. um this is discussion and again, we have two members of the executive committee here, um ((ring, ring)) and I think that, I wanted to give ((ring, ring)) Teresita an opportunity to come in and, and she contacted me last week and she wanted, um, you know, she was under the impression that she was still on the Board of Directors and that she wanted to see about the hours and the change. Um. Let me give you a little bit of history as to what happened here. As you know Teresita was one of the people that was elected at the, at the annual meeting. To serve on the Board of Directors uh. Consequent to that, to that election, we had a meeting that same week, right. I said, you know the board is going to get together, Teresita for some reason wasn't able to come in, um, I'm sure it was a valid reason. And then, the following week I got a call. Jimmy came in and then I, there was follow up by a call to say that Teresita could not make the 8 o'clock meetings and that if the meetings were still going to be at 8 o'clock that she would not be able to serve on the board (LG: oh, o.k.) at that point, um, we I I brought it to Henry's attention, to the board of directors, to the president, that Teresita could not make the 8 o'clock meeting and there was some *discussion* among the board as to (LG: about changing the meeting) about changing the meeting, and changing the days, um (.) and and it was at a board meeting that it was discussed, that Thursday was still the most viable and that 8 o'clock was still the best hour (.) for the majority, um, that's where the communication broke down, if I, if I would say that we should've gotten back, either myself or the president of the board, gotten back to Teresita it's 8 o'clock on Thursdays, that's where it stands now. And assuming, and maybe I assumed wrong or we did. That Teresita was no longer, you know, a board member we didn't do none of that. For 3 months Teresita has wondered why we didn't, she never got any minutes or never got any invitations to the meetings. And so last week, she called me and said are you still having it at 8 o'clock cause I'd like to come (2.0) you know cause we had moved on and had names of other people and we had elected another person to serve. Teresita is here basically to express her concern and and and first of all and most important, she didn't want to be thought of as a person who was irresponsible and a person that didn't care about what was happening in the community, and certainly as a person that didn't want to be on the Board of Directors. She said that was one of the major reasons for running. She wanted to serve. She wanted, 'cause it's interest in the community that she wanted to deal with. I said, Teresita, the best I can do at this stage is have you come to the board, um, you know, explain to them your feelings, hopefully you know, when, unfortunately I was hoping that we would have a full board and that everyone would be able to hear Teresita. But, at any rate, um, Teresita is here and you know, say it how you feel it. (PRC, 2/95 meeting).

Through this introductory preface, the Center Director sets the context for the member's account. First, he notes that the behavior that has occurred has a "valid reason." Then, he suggests that fault may lie with himself or us, as a board. Next, he talks about the reason that Teresita asked to meet with the board, in order that she not be thought of as a certain kind of person. Her stance as a person who "care[d] about what was happening in the community" is a very significant issue (see chap. 2).

Without any pause between JG's preface and her remarks, Teresita began:

Teresita: well first of all I want to apologize for coming here without any notice whatsoever. I did um, decide this morning that I was going to do this. Um, I feel really bad

Organizational Change

because in the beginning, JG had asked me if I would like to be part of the board and um I gave it thought. And um from there, Tomas um, well really JR, called me at home and said Don would like you to be on this board and do you his board, and I said yes, I would love to be on the board but I need to know first, what are the hours. Of the other board meetings that I am actively in, and um, Tomas had said well, because it's a new group, things are going to change and it could be that the hours are going to be changed for the evening. And I told Tomas fine, if that is the case then let me know when in the evening you have the meetings and then like that I can see if I can see if I can um, pursue this board, being on this board. And um, we had the elections, I was, I um, I was elected, I was official and so after that, from there, I was waiting to hear from someone, you know, um, on the board, when we're having the first meeting, uh, what time was the first meeting, uh, nothing was really confirmed to *me*, so 1 month went by and 2 months went by and it was my responsibility and my concern on this board as well as the community that I have an obligation here and I need to straighten out, you know, what is going on here. I met with LG one day and he told me, hey, you missed the first meeting and I met up I think it was someone else, um, you know you missed the second meeting and I'm saying o.k. obviously have me there, why don't they send me the minutes, why don't they tell me what's going on. By that point, being so tied up with this office that I'm working with, it made it very hard for me to get back because my job is this over here, I have to work with these merchants and I have to do and plan all these strategies that a lot of energy and a lot of my time and I decided that um one day being Gomes' office because I had to fax information there he was speaking to JG on the phone, and after you're done with him, I'd like to speak to him and I told J, you know, I'd like to know where I stand here, I feel like I'm still part of this board and what I want to make clear is, you know, I I typed up a letter to mail it in and I never mailed it in because I talked to F and people well hold on the letter and see what happens and I thought that F, somebody was going to send me a letter going on here and then from there and I knew I was going to mail this uh, resignation letter, but I held on to it. And um, when I did speak to JG on the phone the last time I told him, you know I'm really concerned, because wanted to be part of the board but I did not want to be on a board where I was not going to be active um, he said fine, what you could do is, it's no problem, just send in resignation and and that's o.k. you know because I wanted to make sure that the rest of the board understood that I'm not. Um irresponsible here and I I think. (... tape finished and was not reset; PRC February 1995 meeting]

Situational Frame

At the end of this board meeting, the Director of the Center asked those board members who were present to give our attention to a woman who "was under the impression that she was still on the Board of Directors" and who "wanted to see about the hours and the change" that had taken place since her election. This woman was elected as a member of a slate of candidates who were all voted to serve as the new board during the September general membership meeting. However, during the November board orientation session, the Director informed the board that Teresita had resigned because she was not able to "attend meetings on a regular basis" (11/94). Therefore, this account comes after some prior notification.

During this meeting, the Director (JG) situated the account with a lengthy statement that described the ex-board member as having a "valid reason" for her resignation. Because the time of the meetings conflicted with her schedule, we might imply that this constituted the "valid" reason. In terms of sequence, the initial account of being "unable to serve on the board" was given to Tomas (the former board president). Then, the account was told to the current board President. Then, "there was some discussion on the board . . . about changing the meeting, changing the days, um (.) and it was at a board meeting that Thursday was still the most viable and that 8 o'clock was still the most for the majority." Therefore an accommodation was discussed, "changing the time" and then, when the legitimate reason for group action "a majority" decided to meet on Thursday at 8 a.m., "that's where the communication broke down." The blame was laid on a general failure to communicate. More specifically, the Director and current board President "should've gotten back" to Teresita about the decision.

After explaining the circumstances that led to a specific, unalterable meeting date, JG then gave an indication of responsibility by stating, "maybe I assumed wrong or we did." This concession to a shared blame opened the floor to Teresita's later claim that she was left uninformed.

Due to what has been called a "lack of communication," only this board member wondered for three months "why she never got any minutes." Finally, Teresita called and said, "are you still having it at 8 o'clock because I'd like to come."

Because one member had not attended meetings for 2 months, nor expressed to anyone a preference to remain on the board, and because we were informed that she was unable to attend any meetings at all during the November board orientation meeting, the board assumed it had a vacancy to fill. Subsequently, we elected another person to serve in her place.

The account recounted here foregrounds in content and demonstrates, through its telling, the kind of person she was. Even the Director framed the account as a personal statement, ". . . she didn't want to be thought of as a person who was irresponsible and a person who didn't care about what was happening in the community, as a person that didn't want to be on the board of directors. She wanted to serve." In this way, JG affirms the values of the organization and its membership: those who are responsible and those who care what is happening in the community. Even while departing from this board, Teresita's statements reaffirm these values.

To summarize the actions of this newly formed board: There was an "election," the first meeting was called, the time of the meeting was decided among present participants, then monthly meetings commenced. When one board member failed to attend, another person was elected to serve on the board in her place. At some point, "communication" seemed to "break down." One member who expected notification of meetings and minutes, failed to receive them.[81]

Teresita gave an account of her actions. She indicated that her account was warranted, or called for, because of the actions required of one who was elected to serve as a member of the board of directors. Because she did not fulfill her responsibility as a member (by attending meetings once elected), Teresita describes how her failure to so act (as a proper member), has implications for the kind of person she is perceived to be by the other members. JG states, "she didn't want to be thought of as . . ." This positioning is important for the relationships among persons in this community. Explaining gives a person a way to vindicate herself to members whose opinion matters and whose judgment of her actions can color the perceptions of others in the same community.

In her account, Teresita expressed her gratitude for being given the opportunity to make such an account. She expressed her feelings ("I feel really bad") and also about her willingness to serve ("I would love to be on his board") and about the actions and circumstances that led up to the account. She expressed herself as a person who has other commitments ("of the other board meetings that I am actively in"). She expressed her concern for time ("what are the hours").

Then, following the election, she was "waiting to hear from someone" about the time of the first meeting. After not hearing and time elapsed, "one month went by and two months went by" and she admits that "it was my responsibility and my concern on this board as well as the community that I have an obligation here and I need to straighten out what is going on here."

The construction of blame is diffused. Firstly, blame is not place on an individual, but on a group. When Teresita states, "why don't they send me the minutes, why don't they tell me what's going on?" she is not blaming an individual but the group at the Center ("they"). Secondly, blame is withheld. Teresita's intention to offer an account at all is recounted as a spur of the moment decision. She decided to speak to the PRC Director when she was in a room where someone else was speaking to the Director on the telephone. When she spoke to the Director she asked, "I'd like to know where I stand here, I feel like I'm still part of this board and what I want to make clear is, you know, I typed up a letter to mail it in and I never mailed it in cause I talked to [current board President] and people well hold on to the letter." This statement also indicates a vague reference to an indirect culprit, where "somebody was going to send me a letter." Finally, blame is placed on an unnamed person and taken from the account-giver, Teresita who expressed her "concern" for being "part of the board but I did not want to be on a board where I was not going to be active." In sum, she wants to ensure that "the rest of the board understood that I'm not irresponsible here." For all of these reasons, blame is taken off the account giver and placed upon an unknown, vague entity within the Center (perhaps the organization itself).

The preceding account is important to relate in its entirety for a couple reasons. One, there is a way of speaking here that simultaneously takes and denies responsibility. The construction of time lapsing is described as "1 month went by, and 2 months went by." As time is passing, Teresita decides that she has a "responsibility" that causes "concern" for her "obligation." This declaration of personal accountability is very evident and strongly stated. At the same time, finding out prior to the first meeting when meetings will be held was attempted, but then not pursued. Because this line of reasoning is not pursued, we are left to wonder how she constructed her sense of responsibility "at this point." Therefore, responsibility seems to be constructed as something that happens during particular moments. Also, it is something retrospective and as occasioned by a failure to act according to some definition of what it means to be elected as a board member. Part of this definition includes attending board meetings.

Another point that this account establishes is the primacy of relationships within this community. By giving an account, Teresita uses the proper form of communication to try to maintain relationships. The spoken form ("I talked to" and "I spoke to") that implicates personal connection is valued over the less personal, "sending of a letter." However, the clash of these two forms of communication—spoken and written—is pointed to as part of the source of the problem. That is, minutes or notifications were not mailed, nothing was sent from the Center, so therefore, the resignation letter was also not mailed but "held on to." This distrust of the written form,[82] and preference for the spoken, is part of the reason for coming to speak to the board in person, "to make sure that the rest of the board understood that I'm not irresponsible here."

A social breech[83] is indicated by this interaction and the rectification of this breech is achieved in the ritual activity of apologizing. Responsibility and blame often go hand in hand, but in this case, there does not appear to be blame. Blame may be recognized as an indirect consequence for failing to take proper actions as a member. Therefore, what is under scrutiny is one's ability to present oneself as the right kind of person. Presenting oneself to other members as the "right" kind of person is a moral act that implies how our behaviors are understood in business contexts. In such cases, taking an active role in managing one's identity or the perceptions that others hold is the impetus for coming forward to provide an account.

In this case, the accountable act of not attending meetings seems to be overshadowed. Another way to understand the accounting process is that it is a process of positioning members. Those members who count (who are the "right" kind of person) seem to be those who are committed, as evidenced by their attendance at meetings. Those members who have the intention and desire to do the right thing, but who, for whatever (accountable) reason, cannot commit (attend meetings) can be blamed. However, the way that blame for the actions (or failure to act) is done is to ascribe fault to the Center itself, as an organization. The Executive Director can speak on behalf of the Center and its actions. In his comments, JG acknowledges the possibility that responsibility may be shared by all participants (those who failed to send minutes to a board member, who as a result, fails to show up), but it is not the explicit focus of this account. The account is given by an individual member and her inability to share the blame is not achieved.

The narrative[84] begins chronologically. That is, we hear Teresita narrate her story of how this episode began. A key moment in her description occurs when she states, nothing was ever "really" confirmed to me. Here, the idea of personal responsibility becomes slippery. That is, what is "really" confirmed? How did the other members of the board know to arrive at the first meeting? The meeting time and date was scheduled by word of mouth. That is, everyone told everyone else, orally, that there would be a meeting. There was no written confirmation sent out to her, nor any other board member confirming the slate vote and the schedule of meetings.[85]

Teresita did not send in a written resignation first, but rather spoke with the President, and those members of the board who stayed to listen to the account. Subsequently, she mailed in an official resignation.[86] This demonstrated her need, or at least a preference for coming to speak to the board face-to-face. These actions also demonstrate a tension between two channels of communication (oral and written), as well as a difference between blaming an individual versus a group or organizational role category, such as corresponding secretary. These acts demonstrate the preferences of one individual within one nonprofit organization and may also indicate the value of the oral channel and diffusion of blame in such organizations.[87]

What Change is Represented in This Account?

Teresita talks about the possibility that the meeting time and dates might be changed when a new board is elected. That this change did not occur became the primary reason she could not attend meetings. This change is at a very personal level. One person cannot attend a meeting if the time and date conflicts with other obligations. However, the change itself was made by the group. The new board assembled to set the meeting times and dates shortly after the election.

When an individual terminates her association with an organization, we begin to hear statements that indicate that that individual was not involved or included in particular decisions that constitute its membership. In this way, Teresita differentiates herself from other members. Being involved in making a decision about a meeting time is an essential component of what it means to be a board member.

Interestingly, the time of meetings and meeting attendance was not brought up as a group concern. Other members do not attend every meeting and they have not resigned. Other members may arrive late and leave early, and they do not resign because they might be operating on *Puerto Rican time* (Milburn, 2000).

The two changes demonstrated herein illustrate the kind of change that is purposefully engaged in by a group: strategic planning versus the kind of change that is brought about because one person failed to engage in the daily activities of the group: attending meetings.

Summary

The two cases of change cited in this chapter—the change that is purposefully constructed through strategic planning and the change that occurs because of an individual breach—demonstrate two ways that organizations adapt to the ongoing flow of membership.

What it means to be a member is not a static thing. Although individuals may recognize the term *board member* before they join a board of directors, they do not know what the particular requirements of joining a particular board will be. How these requirements become known and worked out in conversation is something that is learned over time and through participation with any given board. Rules do not just exist, they are created and recreated in conversations (Baker, 1997).

Similarly, how one becomes and sustains membership in a board is worked out in conversation. Because conversations are continually in process, organizations may seem to be continually changing. Yet, organizations seem to retain features that appear rather stable. Participants speak in patterned ways that create an organizational culture (Schein, 1991). How members react to what is stable and what is changing is a key feature of the meaning that members make based on what they do. Being able to talk about change in ways that are sensible to others is part of the achievement of maintaining membership.

By taking members' lead when circumstances arise that are specifically noted to be about "change" such as strategic planning or a member leaving, a researcher can listen to these episodes to learn how members talk about what is stable, and should continue, and what can alter about their current situation and circumstances. What is a reasonable account for staying the same or changing is the sense that members make as they speak.

In the next chapter, I share several instances in which members keep track of their talk. These historical records are a mark of stability, rather than change. However, in the production of these records are kernels of both.

Chapter 5

Inscribing the Organization: Documents Structure Actions

Although conversations are often considered the means through which organizations are enacted, any discrepancy between what members say and what they do is often cause for examining the records. Many documents,[88] such as agendas and meeting minutes, function to create a more permanent record of the organization. In fact, organizations are often created by the paper documents on which business plans are first drafted. Like other businesses, nonprofit organizations have mission and vision statements, by-laws, and often, strategic plans (as mentioned in the last chapter).

When new employees are hired, there is often a written job description and it is from this document that later written evaluations are made about an employee's performance. In all kinds of organizations, members are held accountable to the written document. Because of the pervasiveness of written documents, the production of these documents is often viewed as a taken-for-granted activity. One way to understand written documents is by examining the role they play in constructing the facts of what it is to be a member and an organization. In this chapter, written documents are used to demonstrate how participants discuss and come to regard the documents in the process of meetings. My two roles, as researcher and as recording secretary, who produces such documents on behalf of an organization, provided a unique opportunity to describe a tension that exists between taking minutes and referring back to them as organizational history.

What is written down in organizations is not merely a copy of what has occurred, rather how such documents are used in the future actually gives those records *meaning* (see Garfinkel & Bittner, 1967; Gumperz & Cook-Gumperz, 1982). Gumperz and Cook-Gumperz (1982) describe how decisions are put "on record" by creating "written minutes, memoranda, and resolutions" (p. 146). They go on to state that, "such written records and the interpretations they reflect ... serve as the basis of future actions rather than as a representation of what participants may perceive when in particular interactional situations" (p. 146). In order to interpret a meeting and the meaning of any talk within that meeting, participants need to understand the "conventions" (Gumperz & Cook-Gumperz, 1982, p. 159) or discourse forms (O'Keefe, 1981) that prevail in a given social situation. In nonprofit and for-profit organizations, meeting conventions include speaking based on a written agenda, and recording the interaction through written minutes. These two written acts are a significant part of the overall discourse forms within the social situation of a business meeting. Therefore, it is these two written forms: agendas and minutes that are explored for their pragmatic functions within business meetings.

The Use of Agendas

The written agenda, in my experience as secretary, is often created, printed, and copied just before the meeting and does not usually involve the entire executive board. At the FC and PRC the Director and Board President create and distribute to the assembled board a written agenda.[89] The Chairperson[90] of the board is often the one who leads the discussion of the agenda. Because the Director's report occurs near the outset of the meeting, it spans a lengthy period of time and includes many issues about day-to-day business that the Director deems relevant to pursue even if they are listed later on the agenda. Therefore, even though the written agenda does not include a time slot for each item,[91] the director's report can and often does encompass or blend into other items listed on the written agenda. The next item on the agenda, the financial report is often included in the director's report, as in FC, or is given in the Treasurer's report, as in PRC. This financial report is completed quite quickly when board members do not ask questions. Items that require some decision or board action are usually listed next on the agenda—including fundraising events that require board participation to be accomplished.

Boden (1994) defined an organizational agenda "as a talk-based activity through which organizational members pursue local issues, maintain and advance departmental positions and even follow through a stated agenda" (p. 156). Boden's definition does not limit an "agenda" to a written document. However, a written document called an *agenda* is almost always produced, handed out and referred to during the course of the meetings I attended.[92] The written agenda is considered a "playbook" for topics. The president reads the agenda aloud and continues to the next item when s/he deems the topic to be concluded.

During one Family Center meeting, reference to the agenda and minutes were made during the first recorded speaking turn:

1. MF: . . . few minutes go over the minutes because we have some people here for our 20th anniversary brainstorming. Maybe we'll jump to *that* as our second item on the agenda so (.5) gonna stay for the whole board meeting

2. ((cough))
3. MF: need to you're welcome
4. Flip through the minutes maybe that'll help you get an idea of what we've been up to for the last year (11.0) (Family Center, April 2000)

Although at times the approval of the minutes is listed on the agenda, it almost always occurs at the very outset of the meeting when minutes are produced and handed out. If minutes are not physically available to members, approving them is deferred to the next meeting.

Minutes are Referenced

Minutes serve to record conventional information, such as attendance, the time meetings begin and adjourn, speakers, and votes. A set of meeting minutes, then, is both produced and accomplished due to and in the process of meeting. In addition, meeting minutes can be analyzed as discourse acts themselves because members refer to the minutes and also use them to accomplish further interactional goals, such as providing evidence for one's claims.

For instance, during the April 2000 Family Center meeting, the minutes were discussed at the beginning of the meeting. Before engaging in the activity called "approving the minutes," which is the task of having the members vote to accept what is written as representing what was said, there was a question regarding a missing attachment. Next a typo is identified and finally, 3 month's minutes are approved.

1. (9.0)
2. TM: so what I, do we have to approve the last 2 minutes
3. MF: [yea]
4. TM: [um
5. MF: we have to do that two
6. TM: cause I had a question about one of them, remember in it
7. Oh,
8. MF: o.k. go head
9. TM: it said that there was a mission statement attached and it wasn't attached to mine so I don't know if I'm the only one who didn't get the mission statement
10. LB: o.k.
11. MF: we have a mission statement, if you want one we can get you one
12. TM: yea, cause it said it was revised
13. MF: in the official minutes we can make sure there is a mission statement attached
14. TM: thank you, sure
15. MF: yea, we have uh, right up on the wall behind you, but it
16. TM: alright, so that was

17. MF: I think it's that yellow piece of paper up on the bulletin board in the other room
18. TM: motion to approve those minutes hhh hhh hhh
19. MF: why don't we have a motion to accept *all* of the previous minutes
20. TM: o.k.
21. MF: how's that, uh, so are there any corrections or additions to the February
22. Alright, thank you ((papers rustle))
23. (139.0)
24. MF: are there any additions or corrections to the minutes
25. does your copy have a typo over in the second to the last page
26. TM: yes
27. TM: mine does
28. MF: does everyone have that
29. On which page
30. MF: on the last page, there in the middle
31. Here let's get you another copy
32. TM: great, thanks
33. MF: read it, I know what it says
34. TM: yea,
35. MF: o.k., is there, ah, motion to approve the minutes
36. TM: oh
37. MF: we can motion actually to approve February, November and December, is that right T
38. TM: February, November, and October
39. MF: is there a motion to approve all 3 minutes
40. Second (overlap)
41. MF: All in favor
42. Aye
43. MF: All right the motion carries. (April 2000)

This interaction shows how members make reference to two sets of written documents: the minutes and the mission statement. The minutes are spoken of as an object that represents meetings that have occurred during the past months, February, November, December, and October. Initially the request was to approve the last "2" minutes, and then at the conclusion of the sequence, three sets of minutes were approved by a formal vote. The reference to a missing attachment (the mission statement) suggests that the copies of the minutes that members have in their hands are only copies and another version, an official document, exists elsewhere. The minutes seem to be a recorded history of what occurs at meetings and the process of voting is a way to ensure that these minutes accurately record statements made and handouts given during previous meetings. Therefore, when the minutes reference *attachments*, the term refers to what was handed out during the last meeting.[93] The present minutes, as standing for something that occurred in the past, do not have the attachment that was mentioned in them. The President responds to the query by acknowledging the past action (when handouts were given) and for present and future purposes, he describes where the mission statement is presently: hanging on the wall in the room across the hall from where we were seated for this meeting. Therefore, in the conversation, it is worked out that the minutes distributed at the outset of the meeting were not the "official" minutes. Rather, board members held minutes that for all intents and purposes were a copy that could be approved or which stood for the "official" minutes that would be part of the organizational history.[94]

For an example of one set of written minutes that captured the discussion described in chapter 3, consider the first of two full pages of minutes.

Family Center Board Meeting Minutes 2/7/01
Present: Alice M., Kate S. Lil R-M, Kari C, Tracy M. Jennifer S, Lisa B, Andrea F (Guest)
Meeting began at 7:35 p.m.
As a quorum was present, the January minutes were approved.
Director's Report
Jan. 31,2001 $47,484 in Checking Account. CDs had $48,000 (for the first time). Due in part to the JW Foundation, which will pay for long-term expenses: fix computer room, art room.
Cleaning Service: Elizabeth cleans, but not every day. Cleaning service is hired twice per year. Would like them to come in more often, maybe monthly. An estimate has been given for 2x/month for $350, or 1x/month for $200. Could begin in 2 weeks with board approval. (Cleaning: walls, windows, etc.). We have not yet received competitive bids from other services. Commercial cleaners have more equipment than household cleaners. They can come on Saturday, when children are not in building. We could negotiate for $150 and stop during summer. Kari suggested getting another bid before we commit. Taxes were mailed on time (Jan. 15) since fiscal year ends in Aug.
Computer Class: New computers and shelves have been installed in what used to be the library. The curriculum for the computer lab is on the table if anyone wants to see it. Lisa will be speaking to the teacher about it tomorrow to see what we can do for adults (possibly some Microsoft programs and Photoshop). The next session of programs will be for children. We are starting small.
Art Room: The cabinet-maker (Loni S) who built the computer room shelves looked at the Art Room and gave an estimate of $2,300 for a long birch-wood shelf along the sink wall which would have room for storage underneath, with a durable table top (of marble, which is least expensive) and sliding doors (he would build part at home and bring to install here). We have not received a competitive bid for this, but did for the computer room. Loni was chosen because

he was a cabinet-maker, versus a building contractor and Lisa was familiar with his work. Discussion ensued about the benefits of various table surfaces: marble, Corian®, slate, and Formica®.

Lisa will apply to the H & W Foundation again this year for funds to refurbish the Art Room, since they funded us for the last 2 years. We hope to have the Art Room complete by fall. Lil showed us her plans and samples for animal designs by various native people's to be painted onto the walls and rim the windows in the Art Room.

Alice and Andrea made suggestions to talk with art teachers about the various surfaces and their ability to withstand tempura paint, cooking, vinegar and science experiments and the ease of clean up. Kate S. suggested the precut sizes of table surfaces at Home Depot in case ours needs replacing in a few years. Lil and her sister are planning to paint. Kate and Kari volunteered to help. Kari suggested a Saturday spring cleaning. Jennifer suggested that we perhaps schedule a day to complete various different projects.

In this first page, we can see the name of the organization, date of the meeting, the list of those present and the first action that was taken: approving previous minutes. The Director's report indicates the financial status of the accounts as well as some grants that were awarded. The next several segments are topically organized into headings such as Cleaning, Art Room, Computer Classes. These are similar headings that were listed near the bottom of the agenda (after Member Survey, Planning for Board Retreat, and Upcoming events), yet they were brought up by the Director in her report. The next page included summaries under the headings: Surveys, Misc, Staff, Board Retreat, Volunteer Activities, Upcoming Events, and Corporate Sponsors. At the bottom of the page, the date and time of the next meeting was printed.

Compare this, with a set of minutes from the Puerto Rican Center.

Puerto Rican Center
Board of Director's Meeting
Thursday, January 19, 1995
8:00 a.m.–9:15 a.m.

I. Review of Minutes..H.T.
II. Finance Committee Report...L.G.
III. Committee Assignment Update ....H.T.
    (a) Public relations/cultural
    (b) Finance
    (c) Fundraising

        (d) Educational
        (e) Personnel
IV. Old Business .... H.T.
        (a) P.S. Proposal
        (b) J.G./Softball League
V.   New Business.. H.T.
        (a) Board retreat . . . Develop short/long range goals
        (b) Examining Board Membership to PRC
        (c) Possible addition of new committee (youth)
VI. Meeting adjourned. (typed on PRC letterhead, as cited in Milburn, 1998)

The FC minutes were not reproduced on letterhead, whereas the PRC minutes were. The brevity of the PRC minutes is very different from the narrative style of the Family Center minutes. Yet, both indicate who spoke about each topic. In addition, both sets of minutes were produced by the same Secretary. How minutes look, or what gets recorded varies. That the minutes were "approved" by the members of each board seems to indicate that both were acceptable in form and content. The process of approving, or referring back to the minutes can be a discussion that calls attention to their production.

Secretaries Take Minutes

Thus far, agenda and minutes have been described and referred to as objects that exist (Olson, 1981), or have already been produced. Yet, the production itself is important to understand because members play a role in creating these documents, and these roles and products in turn creates a sense of membership and organizational identity.

The production of the minutes is usually accomplished by a recording secretary[95] who is a member of the executive board. Board members elect a President, Treasurer, and Secretary at the outset of a new board. The person who has been voted in as Secretary is responsible for "keeping the minutes" (often stipulated in the by-laws).[96] Although to some it may seem important that this role should require its occupant to have a certain skill set; no requirements were made or asked of me on being elected to this position.[97] Following elections at PRC, an "orientation" session was held for the new board members during which the mechanics of being a board members were discussed, such as use of parliamentary procedure, and so on. By sitting in meetings, listening to what is said and writing down what was discussed, as secretary I was able to produce the minutes. By engaging in these tasks (taking notes and audio recording), the secretary finds herself or himself in a position of recording past oral statements, discussions and votes. These then become official pronouncements by board members when they accomplish activities such as approving the minutes. When written into the minutes, *approving the minutes* or other terms then stand for or represent the actual actions taken by members at a specific meeting. In this way, minutes become a concrete form of organizational history. An organizational artifact is created based on members' speech. When members speak, they know that what they say will be recorded and referred to when the minutes are "approved" at subsequent meetings. However, this act of being recorded can, at times, become the center of controversy (see also Eisenberg, Murphy, & Andrews, 1998).

Learning to take field notes and to be a recording secretary for the first time during my graduate studies was an interesting situation in which to find myself. Garfinkel and Bittner (1967) describe how one reads reports by knowing about the circumstances of their production: who the participants are, how the reports are written, and the initial purpose they serve. Yet, as a reader, one is also in the position of using a report for another, perhaps unintended purpose. It was this quandary that has caused me to continue to mull over this circumstance. As a new member, I did not have the knowledge (sufficient topical competence, nor institutional competence, nor member competence) to be able to write or produce the minutes. Although I believed myself to be lacking in those competencies, I also realized that I could accomplish the task because I did have relevant knowledge and experience (I had taken notes during college lectures). My ability to produce sufficient minutes, for the purposes of this board and this organization, was determined by other members not *before* the minutes were produced, but based on what I actually produced. After seeing what was presented as minutes, members could determine if that information was correct, or not, or if the minutes document contained all of the relevant descriptions of action.

As I came to learn, recording board members' words in the form of minutes serves a very different function for board members than that of taking field notes as a researcher. While as a researcher who is trained in the ethnography of speaking, I often wanted to quote exact words that members spoke and attend carefully to the person who spoke such words, reproducing these words in minutes was considered a mistake. My first attempts at creating minutes with more accountability produced a lengthy 'he said, she said' document that was too cumbersome to stand the place of "minutes" at a meeting (the FC president actually brought this to my attention).[98] It seems to me that it is members' preference (and practice) that printed minutes should take about 1 minute to read; in which they should note the major decisions reached or items discussed during a previous meeting and that is all. If the minutes take longer than that to read, then members complain and the documents are demonstrated to be deficient in fulfilling their intended function.

The power of one who writes the minutes is not often overtly recognized or acknowledged. Although minutes need to be approved, aside from minor typos or spelling errors, it has been my experience that the content of the minutes is not usually questioned.[99] If the content is questioned, then that would lead to a transparent question about the role of the recording secretary, and perhaps indicate a lack of trust in the recording itself. The fact that meetings are recorded seems to create an unspoken sense of importance among participants; and that if they speak, they will be remembered for having spoken. This sense of importance is rare in everyday conversations. The fact that participants seem to rely on a designated individual to be capturing the process of a meeting makes the meetings official and this official business is what makes/constitutes the meetings, organization and sense of membership itself.

Questioning the Secretary's Role

Some board members do not prefer to read the minutes during the first minute of a meeting. During my time at the PRC, there was a lengthy discussion about when minutes are distributed to members.

Another reference to the minutes and the tasks of the secretary occurred in the following segment,

```
466.   HT:      so, is there a motion on the table?
467.   SH:      is there a motion[100]
468.   RM:      I motion that uh, I make the same motion, that agendas
466.            and necessary documents relevant to the next PRC board
467.            meeting be mailed in advance.
468.   TM,FR:   second. (Milburn, 2002, p. 294)
```

During the April board meeting the following discussion ensued about the minutes.

```
427.   JG:  no, I mean, there's no one particular reason, it's just that, and and
428.        again I say that, we have a staff person listening and taking notes on stuff that
429.   HT:  that might be
430.   JG: that pertains to the organization, I say, you know, that, that,
431.        T takes good minutes, it would be incumbent upon us now to send those
432.        on time. I'd rather have a board person here than a staff person here
433.        listening to the business of the agency.
434.   FR:  what about faxing them here? And then, maybe
435.        ((three or four voices begin speaking))
436.   TM:  yea, I normally fax them within a week, but then they get lost in the
437.        shuffle, because, you know, so
438.   HT:  I think we're expecting her to after the meeting, when we go back
439.        to our lives, to sit down and type all this stuff up
440.   RM:  Mr. Chairman, if she's faxing them every week, are you faxing
441.        them already typed?
```

442. TM: yep.
443. RM: if she's faxing them every week its a dead issue. I mean, they're
444. getting here, so they're here somewhere,
445. LG: they're here somewhere
446. JG: yea, no

450. personally, I don't think it should be a st—, board member's
451. responsibility and we all get busy in our jobs and I understand
452. (4.5)
453. SH: so, are you saying, R that a staff person should be in here?
454. RM: yea, I gotta follow the lead of the Executive Director on that, um,
455. and then again, I don't know how the chair, I mean I've been in a position
456. trying to be the recording Secretary and participate in a meeting, you
457. really can't do both, um, that's why I would suggest that a staff person be
458. here, but if the Executive Director doesn't feel that he wants, wants a
459. staff people[101] to see the business of the corporation, even though I think
460. we're subject to the open meeting law, um,
461. JG: well, if we, if we went into, and I say this with all respect,
462. RM:
                    we could
463. excuse a staff person if we go into executive session,
464. JG:
                    I mean, because
465. with all due respect, if we came here and handled strictly the business of
466. the corporation, you know, in and out, it's fine, but sometimes we get
467. carried away talking about things that, that
468. SH: but that shouldn't be it,
469. JG: no, I'm saying,
470. SH: and we should have a lot more
471. discipline,
472. JG: if you, and I don't have a problem with saying to a staff person you
473. need to be here to take notes, but then there needs to be a discipline
474. applied to the board of directors in terms of its business, you know, and
475. and because if we get into other stuff, you know, its only human nature to
476. discuss . . .

Although elsewhere I have described this segment[102] as questioning whether staff should be present during board meetings (Milburn, 1998), this segment also clearly indicates an issue about the role of recording secretary. Several instances include questions about who should take (lines 428, 432, 473) and who should send (line 432) the board meeting minutes. The question of the person who fills the role centers around the idea of including staff in board meetings. The second question concerns specific duties of a person filling the role of Secretary during meetings.

To answer the first question, the conversation centered on questions such as who should "listen" to the "business of the agency" (line 434), who has "responsibility" (line 451), and who has what type of "position" (line 455), who should "see" the business of the corporation (line 459). The second question concerns the following: who "handles" the business, who "gets carried away" (lines 465 and 467), who should have more discipline (line 471, 473), who should discuss what (lines 476), and who's business is being conducted (line 474). None of these questions concern what is written as minutes nor what is sent to whom.

Members learn how to conduct business. When the process of the business is under discussion can refer to two documents, "Robert's Rules of Order" (described by name during at least two PRC meetings) and appeals to the by-laws (made several times at the PRC). That these documents can serve as legitimate references for present actions is significant. One is a published, publicly accessible text and the other is not. This does not seem to matter because they serve a similar function.

Inscribing Conclusions

Writing has been characterized in several ways. Some focus on writing as a context (Kleinman, 1993) within which an organization exists. Others note its functions, including preserving words across time and space, being continually revised and edited, and separating the producer from recipient and text (Olson, 1981; also see Barthes, 1977; Shotter, 1993; Taylor, 2004). Although these characterizations can shed light on the process of writing, they focus more on the act of an individual, rather than the place of writing within organizational life.

Most significantly for organizations is how writing in the workplace creates relationships (Boden, 1994). In this way it matters who the writer is and whose perspective is captured by written records (Garfinkel, 1967; Hak, 1992). While writing can be a "warranting procedure" and put actions into the "public record" (Garfinkel, 1967), its inherent value often goes unquestioned (Pare, 1993).

The role of the researcher as a participant and as a member within organizations has been described by Adler and Adler (1987) on a continuum from shallow to deeply enmeshed. Yet, this characterization only vaguely relies on the role or roles the researcher comes to play in the process of participating. As a sanctioned writer for the organization, the researcher plays a significant role in creating the history of the organization itself. In fact, documents that are produced initially as part of the practical activity of work (Basso, 1974; O'Keefe, 1981; Swales, 1998) often become part of what an organization considers as "knowledge" (Pare, 1993). For instance, Sharrock's (1974) suggestion that researchers analyze specific labels to understand how a group came to know highlights the importance of word choice in creating organizational documents. Not acknowledging this production may lead to what Cicourel (1992) warns, that writing becomes "assumed tacit knowledge."

However, one of the problems has been that authorial voices of the researcher have been muted in the tellings (interpretations of events). This implies a need for or use of self-referentiality to situate the tellings (Rabinow, 1986). Being a member, then, is being part of an "interpretive community" (Clifford & Marcus, 1986) whereby you are part of a group who in interactions gets to decide what previously written texts mean and how they will be used at the current moment of interaction.

Although writing does play a reciprocal role to speaking (Spilka, 1993), the act of writing should be examined because of its significant role in creating and maintaining workplace relationships (Boden, 1994). In this way, we can see that writing is akin to oral forms of communication, in that it "members" and indicates workplace interaction and participation (see also Emerson, Fretz, & Shaw, 1995; Smith, 2005).

Chapter 6

Conclusions: Organization, Communication and Membership

In order to address the three goals of this volume—to illuminate that what it means to be an organization is integrally tied to membership; that communication members organizational participants; and that communicating as members creates the social categories of organizations—I describe some implications for being a member, summarize ways members organize based on activities they undertake, and describe the way members communicate. After these remarks, I reexamine the way members create community before moving on to the methodological implications. Finally, I conclude by urging continued research into nonprofits organizations.

Implications for Being a Member

Employees may or may not be considered, or consider themselves "members" of the organization for which they work. The idea of membership is often reserved for associations we willingly join and, often, for which we pay a fee (such as the sporting associations, camps, or outdoor organizations we may have joined as a child; the fraternal, alumni, or other professional associations we join as working adults). It is these organizations that we join in which we consider ourselves members. Other types of membership are based on community ties. For instance, some people think of their neighborhoods, religions, or cultures as places or groups to which they belong.

The question "Who is a member?" is often determined in a nonprofit membership organization by taking note of who pays membership dues. However, in this book, I have tried to show that who counts as a member at any one particular moment is an ongoing process achieved through communication. Membership itself is integrally tied to the way an organization is described and enacted. Furthermore, membership and organizations are bound to the larger context or community in which they are formed, maintained, and served. In this larger community context, the overlapping boundaries of membership can pose challenges and provide opportunities to the organization itself.

As this investigation shows, members of boards of directors communicate during meetings and other special events. Within these events, organizational members create a local context and it is the task of new members to learn the "local knowledge" in order to effectively coordinate their actions with others in any particular nonprofit organization. This book has been organized using typical "organizational" categories (employees, organizational structure, work activities, change processes, and record-keeping). Organizational scholars sometimes create categories that are different than how work is enacted in organizations. However, by examining these categories more closely in two nonprofit organizations, a clearer picture of *member* categories for their work emerges.

In chapter 1, I demonstrated how membership is created when members name and label themselves and others. The basic building blocks of any organization are the participants. How they come to create and enact certain roles and positions vis-à-vis one another is important for how the work gets accomplished. As we see from these two examples, roles can vary in form from a strong use of titles to a more impersonal use of first names. Phrased another way, both centers had a President and Secretary, yet in only one was that role also used as a title and person reference. Although distinct, these ways of addressing or referring to persons in the organization describe both the relationships among members as well as indicate how members work together (e.g., whether work tasks are conducted informally or structured more formally by following rules and procedures more strictly).

In chapter 2, I demonstrated how membership occurs in a context that is sometimes described by a container metaphor called the community within which a center operates and serves a broad group of participants/constituents. Although any organization can be described as both residing in a community and as potentially having an internal community, focusing on the member description of the label and boundaries of the relevant community is important. It can indicate who is served and why they are served, who is excluded and why they are excluded, who can be a member and who cannot? Geography and ethnicity are the two important features for community in these two centers. Because there is a distinct emphasis on each, it indicates that this feature is not static and should not be taken for granted, but investigated.

In chapter 3, I showed how membership is enacted in meetings whereby individuals coordinate their actions with others to create organizational decisions. Often members are understood as making decisions, but in these cases, the nuances of the decision-making process are important to consider. These nuances can indicate the relative importance of some decisions; they way members create acceptable reasons for their actions, past or future; how decisions are avoided or jointly enacted; and who is responsible for which actions. Furthermore, the idea of everyday rituals helped to demonstrate what was typical across nonprofits, the way organizational rules (such as Robert's Rules) were used to get things done. However, within each organization, participants varied as to their use of the rules to provide a firm or looser structure (i.e., beginning meetings "on time," talk about the need for "quorum," etc.).

Chapter 4 focused on purposeful change conversations like strategic planning and termination to illustrate how a momentary snapshot about what is valuable to members is thrown into relief by the contrast of change. Organizational change is described by the organization literature for managers who want to make work more efficient, but it is not a common topic among ethnographers who more commonly look for enduring patterns that indicate culture. Conversation analysts can be said to focus more on the minute patterns and take an interest in variation that somehow indicates a regulative rule is broken. Knowing that norms and rules can occur on two levels—the interactional level and the broader cultural level and by examining the instances where participants themselves are recognizably undergoing a process they refer to as a "change"—gives us insight into how participants create a sense of their world as both patterned and stable (that which they resist changing) and as temporary and fluid (that which is acceptable to change).

Chapter 5 added a layer of permanence by demonstrating how writing is used to inscribe membership. Although business communication is the arena for those most interested in written discourse, some ethnomethodologists have focused on writing as a site of interest because of the difference between what is said and what is written. Due to the prominence of writing as a feature of worklife, and to the members' indication of writing as a feature of their work, I have included an examination of the way members use writing as a way of making permanent what can only otherwise be held as elusive. It becomes a point of stasis when an organization is made tangible because it has been inscribed into official documents, such as minutes and by-laws.

In this last chapter, I conclude by examining the methodology of membership: using EC, MCA, and EM to achieve a nuanced perspective of these two nonprofit organizations and to learn about what it means to enact membership in such places.

Throughout each chapter, we have seen implications about nonprofit organizations: its culture is created through the communicative practices (organizing) of its members; its communication practices, both oral and written, are constitutive of members and organizations; its membership is more than just a term of identity, it is the relationships that are formed through interaction to create and sustain a community. Findings have suggested that we reformulate social categories from fixed to socially constructed—in conversations and documents—to call attention to the ways that organizational members normalize their practices.

88   Chapter 6

Future research can draw on the methodological approach employed herein to understand the role of social categorizing, organizing and communicating.

Members Organize

When people get together, they organize. In the two centers, the participants themselves "voted in" and labeled designated "board members" who play a central role in organizing the Center. By engaging with other members, board members are positioned as responsible for creating and maintaining the organization of the nonprofit center that they govern. As board members talked themselves and the organization into being, we learned how they used the monthly events of "board meetings" to record and elaborate their work together. Meetings were the places where participants organized the activities of themselves, staff, volunteers, and other participants who used the Center services. This organizational process is the construction of the organization as an entity—larger than any one individual—that goes on before any particular member begins and after any one individual's tenure has passed (both centers are still operating).

It has become commonplace to argue that members organize—but how they organize is a unique enterprise. It is also unique when that organization exists for the benefit of, and through the work of, particular people who also include themselves as members of a particular group, such as mothers or Puerto Ricans. The differences between gender and ethnic identifiers and organizational membership become evident in moments when participants address one another, ask for permission, offer their opinions, and act politely. Although some scholars may suggest that group norms are operating to pattern these interactions, these norms do not necessarily exist prior to their enactment. For instance, when one board member asks, "may I make a suggestion?" during a board meeting, he or she is working to both follow and enact a norm for being a proper board member as well as a norm for working and enacting a nonprofit organization.

Simply put, the fact of being so gendered or ethnic is an unremarkable fact,[103] especially among other members. It is usually when a nonmember (such as a newcomer prompting introductions of participants as "mothers") is contrasted that questions about these membership "facts" in the form of accounts or references to gender or ethnicity occur. When gender and ethnicity are contrasted with what is typical or "normal" among members, then and only then do members note these features.

In fact, it was by studying two nonprofit organizations where I began to learn more than simply what was distinct about each organization, as well as what features were shared across organizations. Although each nonprofit organization is comprised of a unique group of members, it is remarkable how similar are their processes for working together. Therefore, the two centers represent more

Conclusions

than just two case studies, they provide an overview into nonprofit work that is based on patterned practices.

Things Members Do

Both Centers had spring events that were the major fundraiser for the organizations. Often much of the talk during the board meetings was topically related to these major fundraisers. Members were often challenged to demonstrate their commitment to the organization by showing how much they were working on the fundraising aspects. These fundraising activities ranged from mundane activities that went unsaid, such as paying our membership dues or fee to each event, to activities that were discussed during meetings, such as who had gotten the most donations or complaints about our inabilities to go to local businesses to solicit items for auction. Our actions as members ranged from those that were simply expected and unquestioned, to those that deserved or provoked comment. Those that warranted comments had to be negotiated during board meeting discussions. Although a member could simply read a "how to be a board member" book (of which there are several), in order to "know" which tasks to accomplish, learning how to be a board member in the process of being a board member is more than simply an individual accomplishment. These tasks were suggested, required, and expected in order for each organization to exist. It is the work of organizing that forms both the nonprofit organization itself as well as its membership.

When members interact, they negotiate work to be accomplished in each nonprofit organization. This negotiation works as doubly contextual (Atkinson & Heritage, 1984) in that the talk creates conditions for subsequent talk to become relevant. What counts as good reasons for actions creates members whose actions are socially accountable to one another. Those who are able to account for their actions and decisions within the legitimate forms are counted as good members.

When participants create reasons such as personal qualities ("he's nice") or a personal connection with a potential worker, and act accordingly, then they define the nonprofit organization itself. For example, the Family Center is treated as an extension of the home because of its connection to families and child classes and play. It is therefore incumbent on us as participants, rather than researchers, to recognize how members concern themselves with what is relevant for their specific work and not be drawn into judgments about actions based on generic organizational norms.

Although members focus on their fundraising and decision making, they also engage in patterned communication based on the form and sequence of their meetings and events. Although meetings and special events provide places for members to formulate certain actions, such as celebrating community or making decisions, the place and the actions engaged indicate who the members are, based on what they do. So, it is not just that speaking in a particular style indicates an ethnically Puerto Rican way of speaking (Milburn, 1998), or that planning for a Puerto Rican festival clearly demonstrates cultural relevance at a topic level, it is all of the things members do that indicates who they are.

In sum, membership is defined through communicative actions. Consider some of the board member "speaking" activities that constitute membership:

- through speaking in a role (mother/child)
- through pronoun usage (she, him)
- through personal assertions (I am, she is)
- through collaboratively-built utterances (we)
- through the context (community).

Members Communicate

One can seek to understand organizations from a variety of perspectives. Using a combination of Ethnography of Communication, Membership Categorization Analysis and Ethnomethodology (EC/MCA/EM) has helped to make explicit the ways members themselves treat particular interactions as moments of "communication" and the role such communication plays for creating, sustaining and organizing members.

Although it is often remarked that members' actions include communication and that communication itself can be done well or poorly, in this book I have tried to demonstrate that communication itself is a process that constructs membership. Simultaneously, when members communicate (or participate in the process of communication) they are reinforcing/reifying themselves as members of the organization on whose behalf they are speaking (as noted in officially documented "minutes").

Communication is not merely a channel through which information passes. It is not a means for relaying a message. It is all the ways that members symbolically construct meaning. In this sense, communication includes what people do during annual dinner celebrations and monthly meetings, the process of writing and referring to minutes and agendas at meetings as well as the speeches, statements, arguments and justifications spoken by members when they gather together.

Members Create Community

Through communication, then, members talk a larger community into being. Often community is understood as a context within which a business operates. But, like asking about relevant markets, businesses can reposition themselves to include or exclude communities or markets as they change their products or services. Similarly, nonprofit organizations play a part in defining which community they are part of, as well as how that community is formed and maintained. For instance, nonprofit members often hold overlapping memberships and are able to blur boundaries in order to enact a particular community membership at any given time.

Members construct community by participating in specific events, such as monthly board meetings, annual dinners, or spring carnivals. To examine a group based on its government-defined boundaries—a nonprofit organization—is both a researcher's choice and also a resource that members use when they talk. Therefore, the speech community of nonprofit organizations is not an arbitrary label, but an active boundary that members actively use when they speak about their organization as well as define their community.

Members Create Nonprofits

Whereas Sacks' (1992) example of a group whose members belong by virtue of their actions was based on talk from a youth therapy meeting,[104] the groups of concern within this study were generated by the participants themselves based on a larger, governmental definition that exists for such an entity called a nonprofit organization. When board members construct what it is to be a nonprofit organization, they are constructing a public organization. They are participating in a larger social category of work that includes social responsibility.

The idea of organizational culture comes back to the purposefully constructed meanings that participants engage in whenever they interact so as to create patterned ways of doing and being together that obviously (to themselves and others) indicates one organization as opposed to any other.

Methodological Implications

Garfinkel (1967) describes members' ways of socially structuring their worlds, "for all practical purposes." Although members may have routine rituals, or organized sets of rules for conducting their affairs (such as business meetings), how these are conducted in the moment is a very "practical accomplishment" and yet, it can also tell us a lot about the members themselves as well as their culture.

Members categorize not only who members are, or the persons and their roles and relationships, but also the "context" or "setting" within which they act (such as community or neighborhood). They also categorize actions, as good, bad, permissible or in violation of a "natural order" that they have created and are recreating in moments of social action.[105]

Increasingly, those studying gender and ethnicity are turning to membership categorization analysis. Some (like Pomerantz & Mandelbaum, 2005) may consider MCA as a device only relevant in some circumstances and propose Conversation Analysis (CA) as a more encompassing theory and method. However, if you begin by recognizing MCA as a part of Ethnomethodology (rather than a subset of CA), then you get closer to the link to ethnography of communication. Historically, in many texts of ethnomethodology, (see especially Garfinkel, 1967; Watson & Seiler, 1992), authors explicitly described their starting point as the ethnographic experience in order to fulfill the "adequacy requirement." The researcher who tries to learn about and report members' sense-making (Weick 1995) must learn in the process of doing, how members do what they do. Not only does this lead one to discover the labels that members apply to themselves, others and their behaviors, but also it leads one to learn about the patterns that form the "structure" of the organizations within which members work. Nonprofit organizations are unique institutions within which to examine this sense-making because the members are voluntary—they contribute labor and also money they earn at other jobs—in order to help the organization to be what it is and in order to help serve the particular *cause* for which the organization stands.

There is also the question of the scope of one's research. Whereas CA looks at the minutia, and EC looks at the broader culture, there is an interplay between these. For ethnomethodologists, how organizing is done in the small sense is the focus. This work is based on inductive reasoning, examining how individual utterances relate to form a picture of an entire organization. These researchers unpack how what has come to be known as the structure of an organization, is really built in very minute sequences of conversation. In these two centers, we have learned about the whole from the pieces. My focus has not been about individuals, *per se*. Rather, I have used "membership" to focus on the relationships between people in an organization. These relationships, brought into being through communication and inscribed into organizational history, are the organization itself.

Membership is not about individuals in society, but about belonging and being accountable in interactions with others. This definition is based on and implies a particular communication theory. Membership Categorization Analysis serves us well in helping us to look for categories that members use. We see this in chapter 1, when members address one another. There are also action implications for members of particular categories, such as when organizational members "change."

Boarding "Pass"

How members communicate, or how one communicates as a member, has been the main question that the previous chapters have tried to address. Members provide one another with what Sacks (1992) has called "passwords." Passwords are like secret words that allow one to enter a hidden domain. According to Sacks, a password is a word (or series of words) that indicates that one knows how to respond or "answer" in a particular kind of way—the right or correct way. This acknowledgement of a "right way" suggests that words have a previously identified meaning (such as the Family Center's "community" referring to a community mental health movement) and does not focus on the ongoing process of meaning construction that is always at play whenever members speak to continually construct and reconstruct membership in an organization.

Ethnographers are sometimes thought to be researching these passwords, trying to find the keys to understand the behavior of what is going on (see Spradley, 1979). Conversation analysts and ethnomethodologists on the other hand, are looking closely at the process of how things get done. The membership category becomes one instance of a term that is used by members to signify what members do, what members say and who members are—all useful for the entire endeavor.

Philipsen and Coutu (2005) argue that the project of ethnography of speaking is a very broad project that is consistently under both theoretical and methodological revision. EC is a way for researchers to examine cultures and MCA helps researchers to organize what conversational participants indicate when they speak. A reformulation that includes both concepts might be *membering communication analysis*, a new MCA. Whereby what is foregrounded is the members' process of membering through communication and the researcher's joint process of analyzing this process by participating in it.

With this new MCA, researchers would acknowledge their roles as members who participate with others to construct a boundary around what they do through conversation. The act of membering, or crafting an identity through communicatives acts such as addressing one another and accounting for our actions, would be the basis for analysis. This approach would acknowledge the continual process of constructing ourselves and our institutions through communication, rather than be hindered by a limited interpretation about the static being, or past tense pre-existence of categories.

Nonprofit organizations should continue to be a fruitful sight for investigation because the voluntary nature of participation facilitates this kind of reflexivity. Nonprofit organizations are entities that are constructed in communicative episodes.

Therefore, when studying such organizations, it is of paramount importance to examine talk-in-interaction by participating in the life of an organization and by doing the "work." This naturally occurring talk that is located within a business context or setting, or is produced by at least one person enacting an institutional role[106] has implications for the roles, relationships and moral behaviors of those who are organizational "members."

Some future questions one can ask of any nonprofit organization include:

- How does the "social" work that is accomplished become meaningful—or get inscribed/constituted—by members when they talk (which is the work)?
- What communities do nonprofits serve? What group is the customer/beneficiary of the nonprofit organizations' existence? Are members who are being served represented on the board itself?
- How do members describe the "needs" of the community, in such a way as to make their organization sensible to others (funders, donors, the external or larger community within which it resides)?

While reading Fitch's (1990/1991) study of the Columbian ritual *salsipuede* I began to realize that there are two ways to see a nonprofit. Fitch describes the two ways of looking at how someone tries to leave a party. In the first way, one focuses on an individual's attempt to exit the social gathering; in the second way, one recognizes that as people leave a party, the party itself ceases to exist. That is, the group depends on individuals to stay in order to maintain itself as a group. This relates to the idea of for-profit versus nonprofit organizations. For-profit organizations operate under the assumption that pay-for-work is necessary. Nonprofits operate on the assumption that volunteers will donate time (and money) in order to further a cause, or in pursuit of an ideal. By examining the social apparatus or the communication practices of the nonprofit, we can recognize that members participate in pursuit of an ideal without pay. Because participation occurs, a group or a nonprofit can exist. The nonprofit organizational member does not need pay, the organization does not need to pursue traditional business structures; it only needs people who work together in pursuit of a common ideal—that is enough. Nonprofit organizations work because people create the work for which the nonprofit was developed.

Why Continue to Study Nonprofits?

As the nonprofit sector continues to grow, there is also a corresponding growing interest in alternate forms of organizations. Some of this interest is in the form of specific social contexts such as education, health, or the environment. Others are interested in international organizing, in the form of NGOs, whereas others are interested in the new realm of online organizing. These forms of organizing, or creating what some have called "civic engagement," speaks to a growing need to examine how collectively people form and create joint action. The distinct characteristics of nonprofit organizations include its interstitial position that addresses social problems with a particular community focus, where members relate to the organization by acknowledging their contributions monetarily and by volunteering their time. This creates a unique setting for scholars who are becoming increasingly self-reflexive about their own role in their research. Although some scholars have adopted explicit advocacy stances, studying nonprofit organizations is a legitimate way for anyone to conduct research while simultaneously assisting a population in need of a service that might not otherwise be provided (by a government or for-profit organization). I hope that the unique characteristics of nonprofit organizations are refined as research continues into what makes a nonprofit organization distinct from for-profit organizations.

Afterword

Members Run Nonprofits

Directors, chairpersons, or self-designated leaders don't run nonprofit organizations ... members do.

For those who want to take away some suggestions or advice that might help in their nonprofit endeavors, sadly, that I cannot provide. What I can provide is a variety of questions for you to consider as you embark on this work. I have organized them around some key areas where one might likely stop to consider these questions. This afterword will be organized in the following way: What to consider when joining a nonprofit organization; being a member during meetings; taking notes; choosing to maintain or change the organization; and reflexivity for participation. As an individual, you can read and consider these questions, but as a member, you will work together with other members to create the nonprofit organization. Consequently, one must put these thought-provoking questions into action with others in order for them to have any impact.

One: Joining a Nonprofit

The following series of questions may be helpful when you are considering joining a nonprofit. If you are already a member or a Director, then I encourage you to consider your role in facilitating members' discovery of the answers to these questions.

1. *Consider the mission/vision as a statement.* Do you believe in it? Would you write it in another way? Would you be willing to be held accountable to it? As a practical concern, and to assess what it means to the organization, consider when, if at all, the mission statement comes up in conversation?

2. *Consider the roles members play.* These include the formal roles, such as Secretary, Treasurer, Vice President, President and the informal roles, such as volunteers, those who call others or round-up event participants, and so on. When does speaking in that role matter

(within meetings or outside meetings)? Should you occupy an "important" or "official" role? How might that alter the work of the organization? Do not presume you know how to occupy a role to the adequacy of the organization. What does one need to know in order to enact each role?

3. *Consider the context.* What can your read about the organization in the newspaper or in a newsletter? How is the local community described? What are its boundaries? Who is inside versus outside the organization? What is the local standing of the organization in the community? How does each individual contribute to the definition of the community by his or her talk? Is this definition useful to accomplishing the mission of the organization? Might it be effectively enlarged? Who has a stake in maintaining the current boundaries?

Two: Being a Member During Meetings

Because much of the data for this book stemmed from recorded board meetings, I have several comments and questions one can ask about how members participate in meetings.

Board meetings consist of what people do when they are in a room together. That talk itself is work and this work is valuable to creating and maintaining the organization. Knowing this, how should one proceed?

1. Consider how to prepare for the meeting. In order to prepare, don't just decide what documents you need to bring to seem prepared (although that is important), but figure out what *contribution* you can make. Talk to the meeting organizer first and ask.

2. Consider if you should/can invite someone else. Does another person have a contribution to make? Can that person's knowledge, skills, or resources help others to make a decision, complete a project, or consider new possibilities?

3. Consider *your* opinion about a topic and reasons for that opinion. Are those reasons "good" reasons to others in that organization? How can you account for your opinion in a way that is acceptable to the group?

4. Consider your role in the meeting itself. How will you decide when to make your contribution? Will turns be taken "round-robin" or will you have to speak up at a point when something

relevant you have prepared occurs? Thinking not only about the content of your contribution, but the manner of delivery is also an important consideration that impacts how your idea is heard.

5. Consider who speaks most during the meeting. This is often more important than who sits at the head of the table (although these are often related). Who interrupts whom also sends a message (e.g., "I feel my ideas are more important than hers")? Who does not speak at all (e.g., "I may not have anything to contribute to this meeting but my presence can be interpreted by others in many ways")?

6. Take seriously what is said. Although it seems people often work out ideas during meetings, what is said, what is permitted, what is not said, are *all* important features that comprise the organization itself. If others do not take what is said seriously, that is important to try to understand as well.

7. Consider how you will phrase what you are there to say. This is more than just a matter of style—the way you state your opinion, facts, information, ideas, and so on can help participants work together in the meeting or stop it dead. If you experience a lack of uptake for your ideas, consider why that might be? Whose ideas are picked up? How were those ideas or suggestions expressed?

If you offer an idea in a way that puts it on the table for consideration, then others can listen, talk about the idea and incorporate it into what they know and think—the idea then becomes fodder for furthering the interaction. However, making a statement of fact or of certainty does not give others many options but to agree or disagree. They cannot work with the idea or blend it into a version of what they believe. And, the emotions in the room can become stilted.

Three: Taking Notes

When you are in a meeting or working within a nonprofit organization, you may decide to keep notes either for yourself or as the recording secretary for organizational history. When taking notes you should consider several components of the situation.

1. What is typically written down or recorded? What form does it take?

2. Who makes a statement—from what position is the statement made? Who is "involved?" Make note of all participants. Who is a recipient of the services provided by the organization? What is the definition of community? Does the "community" play a role in the organization?

3. Actions—what actions or activities are proposed? What is the level of commitment desired/demonstrated for each action?

4. How do members keep track or record proposed activities? Are these records used for evaluation? When are they referred to or invoked? When are changes made?

5. When changes are proposed at any level (e.g., to written documents, to the organizational processes, to the organizational structure as a whole), who seems resistant? Who wants to maintain the status quo? What does this indicate about the individual's or organization's values? Should written notes capture these tensions?

Four: Choosing to Maintain or Change the Organization

Often, people join organizations because the stated mission of the organization is similar to a cause or goal shared by the individual member. Once a person begins to participate, however, he or she may become frustrated by the way the mission is enacted (or fails to be enacted). When considering whether or how to change the organization to become "more efficient" or more "effectively serve needs," you may want to consider the following.

1. What are the expected or typical versus unexpected transitions? Those transitions that are common and predictable, such as a new event each year (e.g., a 22nd to 23rd anniversary celebration), create limited opportunities for new processes or ideas because they are primarily times for reaffirming a ritual practice. However, a new idea or a change that has never occurred before is more risky to the organization. Because of its risk, some members may resist the change. In order for change to have a successful outcome, it may require more participants to engage in the formation and implementation of the idea.

2. What is reaffirmed when changes are made?

3. What do people want to change that is resisted?

These questions are few and brief because change can be a very tricky proposition. One should listen carefully to what is currently happening, in patterned ways and begin to recognize the areas that are carefully guarded versus the areas that are new or not as well attended that may have room for modification. By considering who has a stake in the status quo versus a new endeavor, you can anticipate who to include in your conversations about the change(s).

Five: Reflexivity for Participation

In sum, being a member is similar to being a reflexive participant in any conversation. One should consider one's potential participation and the ways it fits in with other members. Through this process, you learn more about how the nonprofit is created and sustained.

1. How do members use terms that are familiar to other members?
2. What is left unsaid, because other members infer the rest?
3. How are members recognizable to other members, by virtue of some shared features (verbal or nonverbal)?
4. How do members account to one another for their actions—and are you prepared to give accounts of your actions that are sensible from these members' perspectives (which are always based on a set of shared standards/norms)?

Good luck!

Notes

Preface

1. Exceptions exist to the general trends and I suspect that as the number of internet nonprofits increases, the trend from local, face-to-face service may be decreasing.

2. Historically, this structure is linked in the United States to Harvard University in 1636, where it was first recorded that the "board discharged the first full-time president" (Houle, 1989, p. 4).

Introduction

3. The literature on "social identity" comes closest to this endeavor (Antaki & Widdicombe, 1998; Gumperz, 1982).

4. Although Geertz's (1977) anthropological roots led him to investigate how people do what they do, Garfinkel (1967) was also examining member methods—or how people do what they do—albeit from what has come to be known as ethnomethodology.

5. For instance, Carbaugh (1996) focuses attention on these questions when he suggests examining "communication practices" and "social identity" (see pp. 14–17).

6. For clarification of the distinction between ethnography of speaking and ethnography of communication, see Leeds-Hurwitz (1984).

7. Hansen (2005) explains the split between these two strands of Sacks' work (CA and MCA). Yet in the next issue of the same journal, *Research in Language and Social Interaction*, Kitzinger (2005) describes membership categorization as a "concern" of conversation analysis. This latter article, which is an example of the use of MCA in examining gendering, is also an example of what has been articulated by Hester & Elgin (1997) as the practice in the United Kingdom of not recognizing the distinction between these two areas of investigation to the same degree as "American ethnomethodologists" (p. 7).

8. Arguably, a member must be a person, because Sacks specifies that a member be able to "use" a category. However, it is also important to note that Sacks (1995) did specify that "categories aren't persons" (p. 367), so no one person has one category. A seeming exception is made for children who usually use one category of "family" for everybody.

9. MIR stands for Membership, Inference rich, Representative (Sacks, 1995, p. 41).

10. Hester and Elgin (1997) use the term *mutual elaboration* to mean that each part of the methodological apparatus informs the other part. One only examines a "part" for research purposes, but the parts go together in practice.

11. Drew and Heritage (1992a) describe institutional talk from a conversation analytic framework. However, their definition of what kind of talk counts as institutional is quite informative. They suggest that it is not based on place, but rather, one member must speak in an institutionally oriented way.

12. They do this in order to fulfill the "unique adequacy requirement" (see Garfinkel, 2002).

13. If MCA is about the production and use of member categories, then it cannot be used to fully describe a setting or speech community without combining it with ethnomethodology or the study of member methods. I understand these as two parts of the same coin, where both perspectives are necessary to fulfill the aims of EC.

14. He also includes microanalysis as developed by Goffman. As that is not a concern here, I am not including it among my methods. For fuller explication of the relationships, please see his article.

15. In the introduction, Gumperz (1972) describes the presence of Sacks' and Schegloff's work in this volume as falling within the unit of analysis for studying speech communities called a *speech event*. He states, "speech event analysis focuses on the exchange between speakers, that is, how a speaker by his choice of topic and his choice of linguistic variables adapts to other participants or to his environment and how others in turn react to him. It is this emphasis on exchanges as stressed in this volume by ... Sacks (Chapter 11), and Schegloff (Chapter 12) that distinguishes the interactional approach to sociolinguistics" (Gumperz, 1972, p. 17). It is interesting to note that Sacks' piece "On the Analyzability of Stories by Children" uses membership categorization analysis whereas Schegloff's piece "Sequencing In Conversational Openings" (1972b) uses the sequential analysis that has come to be known as conversation analysis.

16. This could also be a case of creating a category of culture without adequate reference.

17. Although most well known for his combined approaches of ethnography and conversation analysis in *Talking Culture: Ethnography and Conversational Analysis* (1988), Moerman (1974) wrote a chapter included in a volume called *Ethnomethodology* that describes ethnicity as a category, "being Lue." I would characterize his methods as demonstrating membership categorization analysis rather than merely using a sequential form of conversation analysis.

18. This idea of "context" has been addressed by both EC and MCA researchers (see Fitch, 1998, and Hester & Elgin, 1997, respectively; see also Sanders, 1999).

19. Although I am arguing for the use of member labels, I have altered the title of the organizations for anonymity.

20. In the organizational communication literature today, the major topics include culture, globalization, structures and networks, leadership, power, identity, conflict and negotiation, meetings, and decision making (see Jablin & Putnam, 2001).

Chapter 1

21. As Adler and Adler note (1987), the depth of one's membership can vary according to the researcher's or the setting's constraints and affordances.

22. At this time, I was told that some people at the Center were born here in the United States, others moved from the island and traveled back and forth. This "fact" seems to provide another variation on the rationale about not needing to be Puerto Rican, as the population itself is migratory.

23. I also suspected that they chose me at least partially because of my University affiliation as well as my consistent attendance for my twice-weekly volunteer sessions. Unfortunately, this conversation was not recorded. Therefore, the reasons presented and their subsequent act of electing me, I simply counted as fortunate for pursuing my research goals.

24. See Milburn, Wilkins, and Wolf Wilkins (2001) for an analysis of this segment that refers to how researchers' roles are created and "voiced."

25. The staff consists of an Executive Director who runs the daily operations of the Center. The Executive Director has an Assistant. Each component of the Center has a coordinator: Education Coordinator, Cultural Activities Coordinator, and Youth Leadership Development Coordinator. The education component employs an Assistant Education Coordinator, two G.E.D. teachers, a Case Manager, three E.S.L. teachers, an A.B.E. teacher, and a childcare provider, who currently hold courses for local adults at the YMCA. The Cultural component employs a staff consisting of a Folklore Dance instructor, a Gym instructor, a Bridge Building instructor and a Drumming Instructor who hold afterschool programs for middle school children at Chestnut Middle School. The other staff member is the Program Development Specialist who researches and writes grants for the Center and is paid on commission. Three volunteers (including myself) assist with communications, computer programming, and organizing the festival.

26. Formality may indicate that the person being addressed has a public identity (see Irvine, 1979, p. 778). Morris (1981) suggests that "mister" (Mr.) is used in Puerto Rico as a "term of respect...for any man in a superior social position, regardless of nationality" (p. 133). In my data from PRC, formality is based not only on the particular occasion of its use (such as during one board meeting), but is also present during all PRC board meetings. Its presence is always indicated to persons who hold such titles. There is no instance in which someone is given a title merely to continue in that form of address. Although titles are examples of how address is used to indicate speakers and their roles, the use of first names as address and person reference were also used by, and to, other board members. Due to the differences in address use, the formality may be tied to individual participants rather than to the event itself (Irvine, 1979; see also chap. 7 in Leeds-Hurwitz's [1989] *Communication in Everyday Life* for analysis of forms of address in a business context and how they connect to formality).

27. This move of replacing a name with a category is the operation of an M.I.R. device (Sacks, 1989, p. 273).

28. There were three terms of presidency during my research period. The first was a male MF, the second was held jointly between the same male and a female JS, and then the female held it singly (or at least in effect) until the election after I left when she held it jointly with another woman. In this case, it was the Co-President, JS speaking.

29. See also Milburn, Kenefick, and Lambert (2005) for another version of this analysis concerning the role of the facilitator.

30. The whole statement gives the name of the firm, "a firm called ...," which I deleted for anonymity.

31. The presence of turn-overlap makes transcribing the session quite difficult. Some of the speakers are indicated with a single letter, A, B, or C, when their identity could not be deciphered. In addition, without having drawn a diagram of the seating order for this meeting, it is impossible to recall if the speakers used an "around the room" pattern as in the retreat meeting, which was videotaped.

32. The use of first names in this case follows Sacks and Schegloff's (1979) description of the preference for the use of "recognitionals" in reference to persons and in offering one's name as a resource for others to use during introductions.

Chapter 2

33. Discussion of the PRC anniversary celebration and elaboration on the use of the term *community* can also be found in Carbaugh, Gibson, and Milburn (1997).

34. It has been held in local hotels, restaurants, or halls in the same or a nearby city.

35. The PRC also has what's been referred to as a "major celebration of our culture" each summer during their Festival and Parade (2/05). The Family Center has a smaller scale spring festival as well. Both are major fundraising events, but because both are held outdoors and do not cohere around speeches, it is more difficult to describe the discourse during these events. Both festivals were discussed at length during board meetings and this talk has been analyzed for other features.

36. The fluid nature of arrivals and departures can be attributed to Puerto Rican time that operates during social occasions (Milburn, 2000).

37. The keynote speaker used the word "community" 25 times during his 25-minute address. In the previous 5 years, the yearbooks (also referred to as "programs") had the word printed a total of 118 times.

38. Since my fieldwork ended, the Center moved out of the "north end" into another section of the city.

39. When describing community as a container, participants are creating a context metaphor in that context is something that often physically contains (Lakoff & Kövecses, 1987). Using context, then the Center is "within" a community. Considering the language participants use to construct this relationship places the definition of context squarely with interactants, rather than with the researcher.

40. The concept of group identity here is very similar to the way Goffman (1959) described teams: "A team, then, may be defined as a set of individuals whose intimate co-operation is required if a given projected definition of the situation is to be maintained. A team is a grouping, but it is a grouping not in relation to a social structure or social organization but rather in relation to an interaction or series of interactions in which the relevant definition of the situation is maintained" (p. 104). Also consider the significance of the native terms *group of* used within the Annual Dinner, for ways of describing participants.

41. Lines 342–347 are also cited in Carbaugh, Gibson, and Milburn (1997) to illustrate the keynote speaker's inclusion of himself in "our community."

42. Morris (1981) concurs by stating that there is a "discontinuity of individual efforts" that does not impact on the general condition of things (p. 55), which leads to a kind of personal "passiveness" (p. 58).

43. Five years later, they held a 25th-Anniversary celebration. Also note that, unlike the PRC where people arrived late and left much later, most people had arrived for the FC event by the end of the first hour and then left promptly at the ending time specified in the invitation.

44. Although as a researcher, I was curious about the relationship between the Family Center and "community mental health," I am left uncertain about other participants' knowledge or interest in this connection.

45. See http://www.mdx.ac.uk/www/study/mhhtim.htm#WaterTower and http://www.mdx.ac.uk/www/study/mhhtim.htm#CommunityCare.

46. During speeches given in nonprofit organizations, "community" is frequently used as a common topic or "topos" (Aristotle, 1932). Many organizational scholars have suggested that organizations create communities both inside and outside of their building (Burke, 1999; Felkins, 2002; Gossett & Tompkins, 2001). In many cases, speakers describe a community regardless of setting, scene, or audience. Perhaps it is used mostly to accomplish particular goals, such as gaining support and creating solidarity among a varied audience. By invoking a community, one may achieve the goals of gaining support for a common cause among like-minded individuals who now see themselves as part of a community. In fact, this might incidate *topos* 12, arguing from the parts to the whole (Aristotle, 1932, p. 165).

47. Both of whom build on Turner's (1967) definition of ritual.

48. Similarly, Knuf (1993) described one of the functions of ritual was to separate members from nonmembers.

49. In its larger sense, institutions *as* context, has been discussed by Katriel (1995) and Drew & Heritage (1992b).

50. This process fulfills Garfinkel's (2002) "unique adequacy requirement" (pp. 72, 175).

51. Pearce and Pearce (2004) describe context as a container within which communication occurs.

52. Goffman (1967), whose research has strands that are connected to EC and CA, limits ritual to symbolic acts that show respect. Throughout his monograph, he describes ritual games, ritual interactions, and ritual order as patterned ways of acting. Although many rituals may be concerned with how individuals maintain face with one another, that is not the only function they serve.

Chapter 3

53. I wish to thank George Cheney and Stuart Sigman for their helpful comments about the segment used in this chapter when it was part of a data session at NCA.

54. Those who consider the goal of meetings to be "decision making" may be following the "rationale actor" model that Conrad and Poole (2002) decry.

55. Weitzel and Geist (1998) describe the way one community group uses Parlimentary Procedure. Although there are "rules," how these rules are interpreted and enacted varies depending on the situation.

56. Often by saying "um" as Boden (1994) notes.

57. After the first year of my involvement with the board, co-presidents were selected. Only one of the co-presidents would run each meeting.

58. An exception to this was the transition to the last Co-President of my tenure. During that meeting, the pause was so lengthy (nearly 82 seconds) and the procedure for what would happen next did not flow as "naturally" as it had during previous meetings. In fact, the new "chair" had to be told what to do, "do you want to make a nomination that the person accept; you're chair."

This followed a sequence clarifying this role, that wasn't being enacted.

JS: she's going to chair the meeting
SW: does anyone move to approve the minutes?
AM: I will
(3.0)
SW: the director's report, would that be part of the minutes?
LB: it's separate
SW: ok.

59. To my knowledge, an external financial advisor was never engaged.

60. The format of the agenda was the same as appears here: a one page, typewritten, white piece of paper with exactly the words shown here was handed out.

61. I believe it is safe to assume that none of the members had professional experience with cabinets or countertops—given the biographies they presented during board elections and that no one made that claim during this, or other, discussions.

62. One notion to consider is the role of "groupthink" (Janis, 1972) during this meeting. That theory suggests that a leader is in a strong position to influence the group to move towards some consensus (also see Seibold, Meyers, & Sunwolf, 1996). In this group, the person with the most speaking time and the most seniority (17 years) is the Director. There is also significant influence by the President of the board who guides the direction that the conversation in the meetings takes (by referring to the agenda, and "moving on" to the next topic). In this segment, JS evaluates the previous statement, "sounds good" and then follows up with a statement about the "price," which also doesn't sound "too bad." That is a way of officially sanctioning a decision. For instance, one could claim that by using official speak from her position as Co-President, JS helps to make a decision out of much talk that continues. She says we can "vote" on it.

63. M1-4 indicates unknown speakers because they were difficult to distinguish during transcription.

64. There are several instances of discussions about "money" (10 instances from May 2000–Oct. 2001), other references were made to expenses, cost, price, and dollars, but they do not have the same weight for participants, as evidenced by less talk time, less elaboration, and less frequency.

65. This kind of pattern has been described as an American form (Carbaugh, 1989, 2002).

66. Dewey's (1910) six-step problem solving method includes: defining the problem, analyzing the problem, creating criteria to judge solutions, listing alternatives, evaluating solutions, and choosing the best (as cited in Hoover, 2002).

67. As defined in their by-law, a quorum constituted one more than half; in other words, a simple majority.

68. From a recorded corpus of 28 total.

Notes

69. In Milburn (2000), I reference lines 413–416 to illustrate members' use of Puerto Rican time.

70. Weick (1995) cites Garfinkel's work with jurors in the 1960s, when he talked about how Garfinkel examined the deliberations and found that the jurors first decided on the outcome and then brought up the facts that concurred with their decided outcome.

71. In fact, Garfinkel (1967) talked about defining decisions retrospectively before Weick did. See previous footnote for Weick's acknowledgement of this work.

Chapter 4

72. Large meetings may use a "future search process," whereas small meetings may be limited to one department or even a two-person, supervisor-employee personal development meeting.

73. During the years from 1995–1999, I worked in another nonprofit organization where this occurred. During the process, every employee had to become "rehired" into new positions or leave the organization.

74. Trice and Beyer (1984) described several change events, among which were included specific rites like rites of passage, enhancement, as well as termination.

75. Organizational developers or meeting facilitators often advise organizational members to hold these meetings at an alternate, off-site location.

76. I had worked with this facilitator on a number of other group and organizational development projects.

77. I am grateful to Hampton Press for giving permission to use this excerpt from Frey's (2005) text, Facilitating Group Communication.

78. The retreat was held in the morning and lasted approximately 5 hours, whereas the monthly board meetings were all held in the evening and were usually completed within 2 hours.

79. In business literature, this is called the "core competencies" of a company (Prahalad & Hamel, 1990).

80. The achievement of quorum varies during any given meeting and changes during any one meeting.

81. Interestingly, this topic of "failing" to receive the minutes and agenda before meetings was a topic during one board meeting—yet, at that meeting; the fact of this failure did not prevent other board members from attending (nor did anyone connect the two incidents during either discussion).

82. The significance of written documents will be picked up again in the next chapter

83. Turner (1969) describes rituals that are enacted because someone has failed to fulfill a "social obligation."

84. See Czarniawska (1997) for a kind of organizational narrative.

85. One could argue that it was the responsibility of the recording Secretary (i.e., my "fault"). I was never blamed.

86. I never saw this official resignation letter; presumably it was sent to the Director and given to the President of the Board.

87. Supporting research by Berk-Seligson indicates that grammatical constructions are used "to avoid attribution of blame to persons in adverse situations" (Brown & Levinson, p. 27). Although she studied Costa Rican Spanish particularly, she suggests that her findings are more widespread among North American Spanish speakers.

Chapter 5

88. Trice and Beyer (1984) use the term *artifacts* to refer to "material objects" that "facilitate culturally expressive activity" (p. 655). I prefer to use the term *documents*, because it is a member term in use within business discourse, rather than an anthropological or researcher term that examines a culture as an other.

89. Although the preparation and distribution of a written agenda may seem so commonplace as to not warrant comment, I refer the reader to Duranti (1994), who describes a Samoan *fono* where an agenda is more of an abstract story to be worked out in the telling (see p. 120).

90. *President* and *Chairperson* are used interchangeably here.

91. As one can find on an agenda template in software packages such as MS Word.

92. The exceptions were the two strategic planning events whereby the facilitator asked participants to articulate a number of goals that they wanted to see the organization achieve, and to state what part they were willing to play in achieving these goals. For instance, following their introductory remarks, participants talked at length about the ideas they had and the interests they brought to the organization. The areas that members identified became the basis for the plans made for the organization. By making public individual agendas at the outset, participants constructed an organizational agenda that they all shared. This was one case whereby the agenda became a living, consciously co-constructed plan.

93. I had not attended that previous meeting when I asked for a copy of the mission statement.

94. I do not know where these are or who decides that they are "official."

95. Robert's Rules of Order also allow for a corresponding secretary (see Patnode, 1989). There was only one "secretary" position in both boards. In fact, I have only been on one board that had both positions filled.

96. In the PRC, the by-laws stipulate actions that the board of directors should take. I describe this in Milburn (1998, emphasis added),

"These duties include:
1. To see it that the resolutions of the Board are carried out.
2. To approve a yearly work plan.
3. To maintain an inventory of the physical facilities and resources of the corporation.
4. To receive the goods and funds for the corporation.
5. To approve a yearly finance budget.
6. To hold a meeting once a month or as often as necessary. (Half plus one of the members constitutes a quorum).

7. To receive and make real the bank account of the Puerto Rican Center, Inc. or to open one, if there is none.
8. To conduct an official and permanent direction, and to present it to the citizens in general at the annual meeting or when inquiry is made.
9. To request from each Special Committee a yearly plan of work of its specific area.
10. *To keep the official book of the minutes.*
11. Each Board Member shall serve on at least one standing committee.
12. The Board of Directors terminating should present to the one taking over all the documents and belongings of the Puerto Rican Center, Inc. in a meeting called to this effect 10 (ten) days from the election of the said Board. (Section IV)."

97. Perhaps presumptions were made about my skills because members knew I was an academic pursuing research in the writing of my doctoral dissertation.

98. This conversation took place as a side conversation, not part of the recorded meetings.

99. I do have one instance from a PTA meeting whereby the current meeting's minutes include a reference to what was voted to be changed in the previous minutes due to what some considered an unflattering characterization of one of the participants.

100. This was not an instance of turn overlap.

101. This section, like all others, was transcribed as it was recorded: The article and object are not in agreement as spoken.

102. This segment was used to discuss research reflexivity in Milburn, Wilkins, and Wolf Wilkins (2001).

Chapter 6

103. A similar idea was initially posited by Garfinkel (1967) in his discussion about Agnes' gender work.

104. For Sacks (1992), "hotrodders" were the group of members who belong by virtue of their actions, such as, driving a Boneville, or looking a certain way at a guy.

105. Garfinkel (1967) also refers to this as "*ad hocing.*"

106. Drew and Heritage (1992) describe institutional talk as interaction that occurs between two people, one of whom is recognizably an institutional member. Heritage (2005) describes three components of institutional talk, (1) the goals are institutionally relevant, (2) the business presents specific constraints on the interaction, (3) interpretations [of meaning] depend upon the "institutional context" (see p. 106, and also Drew & Heritage, 1992).

References

Adler, P. A., & Adler, P. (1987). *Membership roles in field research.* Newbury Park, CA: Sage.
Albert, S., & Whetten, D. A. (1985). Organizational identity. *Research in Organizational Behavior, 7,* 263–295.
Antaki, C., & Whitticomb, S. (Eds.). (1998). *Identities in talk.* London: Sage.
Aristotle (1932). *The Rhetoric of Aristotle* (L. Cooper, Trans.). Englewood Cliffs, NJ: Prentice Hall.
Atkinson, J. M., & Heritage, J. (1984). *Structures of social action: Studies in conversation analysis.* Cambridge, UK: Cambridge University Press.
Bailey, B. (1997). Communication of respect in interethnic service encounters. *Language in Society, 26,* 327–356.
Bakan, J. (2004). *The corporation: The pathological pursuit of profit and power.* New York: Free Press.
Baker, C. (1997). Ticketing rules: Categorization and moral ordering in a school staff meeting. In S. Hester & P. Elgin (Eds.), *Culture in action: Membership categorization analysis* (pp. 77–98). Boston: University Press of America.
Barthes, R. (1977). The death of the author. In S. Heath (Ed. & Trans.)., *Image, music, text.* New York: Hill.
Basso, K. H. (1974). The ethnography of writing. In R. Bauman & J. Sherzer (Eds.) *Explorations in the ethnography of speaking* (pp. 425–432). Cambridge, MA: Cambridge University Press.
Basso, K. H. (1988). 'Speaking with names': Language and landscape among the Western Apache. *Cultural Anthropology, 3,* 99–130.
Baumann, G. (1996). *Contesting culture: Discourses of identity in multi-ethnic London.* Cambridge, UK: Cambridge University Press.
Berry, J. M. (2003). *A voice for nonprofits.* Washington, DC: Brookings Institution Press.
Boden, D. (1994). *The business of talk: Organizations in action.* Cambridge, UK: Polity Press.
Bridges, W. (1991). *Managing transitions.* Reading, MA: Addison-Wesley.
Brown, P., & Levinson, S. C. (1978). *Politeness: Some universals in language usage.* Cambridge, UK: Cambridge University Press.
Burke, E. M. (1999). *Corporate community relations: The principle of the neighbor of choice.* Westport, CT: Praeger.
Buttny, R. (1993). *Social accountability in communication.* London: Sage.

Buttny, R. (2004). *Talking problems: Studies of discursive construction*. Albany: State University of New York Press.
Carbaugh, D. (1985). Cultural communication and organizing. In W. B. Gudykunst, L. P. Stewart, & S. Ting-Toomey (Eds.), *Communication, culture, and organizational processes*. Beverly Hills: Sage.
Carbaugh, D. (1988). Cultural terms and tensions in the speech at a television station. *Western Journal of Speech Communication, 52*, 216–237.
Carbaugh, D. (1989). *Talking American: Cultural discourses on Donahue*. Norwood, NJ: Ablex.
Carbaugh, D. (1993). Personhood, positioning, and cultural pragmatics: American dignity in cross-cultural perspective. In S. Deetz (Ed.), *Communication yearbook 17* (pp. 159–186). Thousand Oaks, CA: Sage.
Carbaugh, D. (2002). Some distinctive features of US American conversation. In W. Eadkie & P. Nelson (Eds.), *The changing conversation in America* (pp. 61–75). Thousand Oaks, CA: Sage.
Carbaugh, D. (1996). *Situating selves: The communication of social identities in American scenes*. Albany: State University of New York Press.
Carbaugh, D. (2005). *Cultures in conversation*. Mahway, NJ: Erlbaum.
Carbaugh, D., Gibson, T. A., & Milburn, T. (1997). A view of communication and culture: Scenes in an ethnic cultural center and a private college. In B. Kovacic (Ed.), *Emerging theories of human communication* (pp. 1–24). Albany: State University of New York Press.
Cheney, G. (1991). *Rhetoric in an organizational society: Managing multiple identities*. Columbia: University of South Carolina Press.
Cicourel, A. V. (1992). The interpenetration of communicative contexts: Examples from medical encounters. In A. Duranti & C. Goodwin (Eds.), Rethinking context: Language as an interactive phenomenon (pp. 291–310). Cambridge, UK: Cambridge University Press.
Clifford, J., & Marcus, G. E. (1986). *Writing culture: The poetics and politics of ethnography*. Berkeley: University of California Press.
Conrad, C., & Poole, M. S. (2002). *Strategic organizational communication: In a global economy* (5th ed.). Fort Worth, TX: Harcourt College Publishers.
Covarrubias, P. (2002). *Culture, communication and cooperation: Interpersonal relations and pronominal address in a Mexican organization*. Lanham, MD: Rowan & Littlefield.
Czarniawska, B. (1997). *Narrating the organization: Dramas of institutional identity*. Chicago: The University of Chicago Press.
Deal, T. E., & Kennedy, A. A. (1982). *Corporate cultures: The rites and rituals of corporate life*. Reading, MA: Addison-Wesley.
Deetz, S., & Simpson, J. (2004). Critical organizational dialogue: Open formation and the demand of otherness. In R. Anderson, L. A. Baxter, & K. N. Cissna (Eds.), *Dialogue: Theorizing difference in communication studies* (pp. 141–158). Thousand Oaks, CA: Sage.
Drew, P., & Heritage, J. (1992a). Analyzing talk at work: An introduction. In P. Drew & J. Heritage (Eds.), *Talk at work: Interaction in institutional settings* (pp. 5–62). Cambridge, UK: Cambridge University Press.
Drew, P., & Heritage, J. (1992b). *Talk at work: Interaction in institutional settings*. Cambridge, UK: Cambridge University Press.

Drucker, P. (July–Aug. 1989). What business can learn from nonprofits. *Harvard Business Review, 67*(4), 88–94.
Drucker, P. (2001). *Managing the nonprofit organization.* Oxford, UK/MA: Butterworth-Heinemann.
Duca, D. J. (1996). *Nonprofit boards: Roles, responsibilities and performance.* New York: Wiley.
Duranti, A. (1994). *From grammar to politics: Linguistic anthropology in a Western Samoan Village.* Berkeley: University of California Press.
Eckert, P. (1989). *Jocks and burnouts: Social categories and identity in the high school.* New York: Teachers College Press.
Eisenberg, E. M., Murphy, A., & Andrews, L. (1998). Openness and decision making in the search for a university provost. *Communication Monographs, 1,* 1–24.
Elsbach, K. D., & Kramer, R. M. (1996). Members' responses to organizational identity threats: Encountering and countering the *Business Week* rankings. *Administrative Science Quarterly, 41,* 442–468.
Emerson, R. M., Fretz, R. I., & Shaw, L. L. (1995). *Writing ethnographic fieldnotes.* Chicago: The University of Chicago Press.
Felkins. P. K. (2002). *Community at work: Creating and celebrating community in organizational life.* Cresskill, NJ: Hampton Press.
Fitch, K. (1990/1991). A ritual for attempting leave-taking in Columbia. *Research in Language and Social Interaction* [Special Section: Ethnography and Conversation Analysis after Talking Culture], *24,* 209–224.
Fitch, K. (1998). Text and context: A problematic distinction in ethnography. *Research in Language and Social Interaction, 31,* 91–107.
Frost, P. J., Moore, L. F., Reis Louis, M., Lundberg, C. C., & Martin, J. (Eds.). (1991). *Reframing organizational culture.* Newbury Park, CA: Sage.
Frumkin, P. (2002). *On being nonprofit: A conceptual and policy primer.* Cambridge, MA: Harvard University Press.
Garfinkel, H. (1967). *Studies in ethnomethology.* Englewood Cliffs, NJ: Prentice-Hall.
Garfinkel, H. (Ed.). (1986). *Ethnomethodological studies of work.* London: Routledge & Kegan Paul.
Garfinkel, H. (2002). *Ethnomethodologist's program: Working out Durkheim's aphorism.* Lanham, MD: Rowman & Littlefield.
Garfinkel, H., & Bittner, E. (1967). Good organizational reasons for bad clinical records. In H. Garfinkel (Ed.), *Studies in ethnomethology.* Englewood Cliffs, NJ: Prentice-Hall.
Garfinkel, H., & Sacks, H. (1986). On formal structures of practical actions. In H. Garfinkel (Ed.), *Ethnomethodological studies of work* (pp. 160–193). London: Routledge & Kegan Paul.
Geertz, C. (1977). "From the native's point of view": On the nature of anthropological understanding. In J. L. Dolgin, D. S. Kemnitzer, & D. M. Schneider (Eds.), *Symbolic anthropology: A reader in the study of symbols and meanings* (pp. 221–237). New York: Columbia University Press.
Girton, G. D. (1986). Kung fu: Toward a praxiological hermeneutic of the martial arts. In H. Garfinkel (Ed.), *Ethnomethodological studies of work* (pp. 60–91). London: Routledge & Kegan Paul.
Glenn, P., LeBaron, C. D., & Mandelbaum, J. (Eds.). (2003). *Studies in language and social interaction.* Mahwah, NJ: Erlbaum.

Goffman, E. (1959). *The presentation of self in everyday life*. Garden City, NY: Doubleday Anchor Books.
Goffman, E. (1967). *Interaction ritual: Essays on face-to-face behavior*. Garden City, NY: Anchor Books.
Goffman, E. (1974). *Frame analysis*. New York: Harper & Row.
Gossett, L. M., & Tompkins, P. K. (2001). Community as a means of organizational control. In G. J. Shepherd & E. W. Rothenbuhler (Eds.), *Communication and community* (pp. 111–133). Mahwah, NJ: Erlbaum.
Goodwin, C., & Duranti, A. (1992). *Rethinking context: Language as an interactive phenomenon*. Cambridge, UK: Cambridge University Press.
Gumperz, J. J. (1972). Introduction. In J. J. Gumperz & D. Hymes (Eds.), *Directions in sociolinguistics: The ethnography of communication* (pp. 1–25). New York: Holt, Rinehart and Winston.
Gumperz, J. J. (Ed.). (1982). *Language and social identity*. Cambridge, UK: Cambridge University Press.
Gumperz, J. J., & Cook-Gumperz, J. (1982). Interethnic communication in committee negotiations. In J. Gumperz (Ed.), *Language and social identity* (pp. 145–162). Cambridge, UK: Cambridge University Press.
Gumperz, J. J., & Hymes, C. (Eds.). (1972). *Directions in sociolinguistics: The ethnography of communication*. New York: Holt, Rinehart and Winston.
Hak, T. (1992). Psychiatric records as transformation of other texts. In G. Watson & R. M. Seiler (Eds.), *Text in context: Contributions to ethnomethodology* (pp. 138–155). Newbury Park, CA: Sage.
Hall, B. J. (1997). Ritual as part of everyday life. In J. Martin, T. K. Nakayama, & L. A. Flores (Eds.), *Readings in cultural contexts* (pp. 172–179). Mountain View, CA: Mayfield Publishing Company.
Hamel, G., & Prahalad, C. (1996). *Competing for the future*. Boston, MA: Harvard Business School Press.
Hansen, A. D. (2005). A practical task: Ethnicity as a resource in social interaction. *Research in Language and Social Interaction, 38*(1), 63–104.
Heritage, J. (2005). Conversation analysis and institutional talk. In R. E. Sanders & K. L. Fitch (Eds.), *Handbook of language and social interaction* (pp. 103–147). Mahwah, NJ: Erlbaum.
Hester, S. P., & Eglin, P. (Eds.). (1997). *Culture in action: Studies in membership categorization analysis*. Washington, DC: University Press of America.
Hogg, M. A., & Terry, D. J. (2000). Social identity and self-categorization processes in organizational contexts. *Academy of Management Review, 25*, 121–140.
Hogg, M. A., Terry, D. J., & White, K. M. (1995). A tale of two theories: A critical comparison of identity theory with social identity theory. *Social Psychology Quarterly, 58*, 255–269.
Holtgraves, T. M. (2002). *Language as social action: Social psychology and language use*. Mahwah, NJ: Erlbaum.
Hoover, J. D. (2002). *Effective small group and team communication*. Fort Worth, TX: Harcourt College Publishers.
Hopper, R., & LeBaron, C. (1998). How gender creeps into talk. *Research in Language and Social Interaction, 31*(1), 59–74.

Houle, C. O. (1989). *Governing boards: Their nature and nurture*. San Francisco: Jossey-Bass.

Housley, W. & Fitzgerald, R. (2002). The reconsidered model of membership categorization analysis. *Qualitative Research, 2*(1), 59–83.

Hymes, D. (1962). The ethnography of speaking. In T. Gladwin & W. Sturtevant (Eds.), *Anthropology and human behavior* (pp. 13–53). Washington, DC: Anthropological Society of Washington.

Hymes, D. (1972). Models of the interaction of language and social life. In J. Gumperz & D. Hymes (Eds.), *Directions in sociolinguistics: The ethnography of communication* (pp. 35–71). New York: Holt, Rinehart, & Winston.

Hymes, D. (1974). *Foundations in sociolinguistics: An ethnographic approach*. Philadelphia: University of Pennsylvania Press.

Internal Revenue Service: United States Department of the Treasury. Tax information for other nonprofits. Retrieved June 24, 2006, from http://www.irs.gov/charities/nonprofits/index.html

Irvine, J. T. (December 1979). Formality and informality in communicative events. *American Anthropologist, 81*(4), 773–790.

Jablin, F. M., & Putnam, L. L. (2001). *The new handbook of organizational communication: Advances in theory, research, and methods*. Thousand Oaks, CA: Sage.

Janis, I. L. (1972). *Victims of groupthink*. Boston: Houghton Mifflin.

Kanter, R. M., Stein, B., & Jick, T. (1992). *The challenge of organizational change*. New York: Free Press.

Katriel, T. (1995). From "context" to "contexts" in intercultural communication research. In R. L. Wiseman (Ed.), *Intercultural communication theory*. Thousand Oaks, CA: Sage.

Kitzinger, C. (2005). "Speaking as a heterosexual": (How) does sexuality matter for talk-in-interaction? *Research in Language and Social Interaction, 38*(3), 221–265.

Kleinman, S. (1993). The reciprocal relationship of workplace culture and review. In R. Spilka (Ed.), *Writing in the workplace: New research perspectives* (pp. 56–70). Carbondale: Southern Illinois University Press.

Knuf, J. (1993). "Ritual" in organizational culture theory: Some theoretical reflections and a plea for greater terminological rigor. In S. A. Deetz (Ed.), *Communication yearbook, 16* (pp. 61–103). Thousand Oaks, CA: Sage.

Kotter, J. (1996). *Leading change*. Boston, MA: Harvard Business School Press.

Lakoff, G., & Johnson, M. (1980). *Metaphors we live by*. Chicago: University of Chicago Press.

Lakoff, G., & Kövecses, Z. (1987). *The cognitive model of anger inherent in American English*. Cambridge, UK: Cambridge University Press.

Leeds-Hurwitz, W. (1984). On the relationship of the "ethnography of speaking" to the "ethnography of communication." *Papers in Linguistics: International Journal of Human Communication, 17,* 7–32.

Leeds-Hurwitz, W. (1989). *Communication in everyday life: A social interpretation*. Westport, CT: Greenwood Publishing Group.

Leeds-Hurwitz, W. (2002). *Wedding as text: Communicating cultural identities through ritual*. Mahwah, NJ: Erlbaum.

Lepper, G. (2000). *Categories in text and talk*. London: Sage.

Marcus, G. E. (1986). Contemporary problems of ethnography in the modern world system. In J. Clifford & G. E. Marcus (Eds.), *Writing culture: The poetics and politics of ethnography* (pp. 165–193). Berkeley: University of California Press.

Milburn, T. (1998) *Conversation and culture in the Puerto Rican Cultural Center: An ethnographic exploration of communicating personhood.* Unpublished doctoral dissertation, University of Massachusetts, Amherst.

Milburn, T. (2000). Enacting 'Puerto Rican time' in the United States. In M. J. Collier (Ed.), *Constituting cultural difference through discourse: The international and intercultural communication annual, 23,* 47–76. Thousand Oaks, CA: Sage.

Milburn, T. (2002). Collaboration and the construction of Puerto Rican community. In M. P. Orbe, T. McDonald, & T. Ford-Ahmed (Eds.), *Building diverse communities* (pp. 287–303). Cresskill, NJ: Hampton Press.

Milburn, T. (2004). Speech community: Reflections upon communication. *Communication yearbook, 28,* 411–441.

Milburn, T., Kenefick, J., & Lambert, A. (2005). Facilitating a Board of Directors' Planning Retreat: Not-for-Profit Sensemaking. In L. Frey (Ed.), *Facilitating group communication: Innovations and applications with natural groups* (Vol. 2, pp. 3–28). Cresskill, NJ: Hampton Press.

Milburn, T., Wilkins, R., & Wolf Wilkins, K. (2001). Reflexive moments: Negotiating researcher roles in participant observation. *Iowa Journal of Communication, 33,* 106–123.

Mintzberg, H. (1994). *The rise and fall of strategic planning.* New York: The Free Press.

Moerman, M. (1974). Accomplishing ethnicity. In R. Turner (Ed.), *Ethnomethodology: Selected readings* (pp. 54–68). Middlesex, UK: Penguin Education. (Original work published 1968)

Moerman, M. (1988). *Talking culture: Ethnography and conversation analysis.* Philadelphia: University of Pennsylvania Press.

Morris, M. (1981). *Saying and meaning in Puerto Rico: Some problems in the ethnography of discourse.* New York: Pergamon Press.

National Mental Health Association. (2006). *NMHA and the history of the mental health movement.* Retrieved January 12, 2006, from http://www.nmha.org/about/history.cfm

NCCS Data Web. (2006). Number of nonprofit organizations in the United States 1996–2004. Retrieved March 24, 2006, from http://nccsdataweb.urban.org/PubApps/profile1.php?state=US

O'Keefe, B. J. (1981). Writing, speaking and the production of discourse. In B. M. Kroll & R. J. Vann (Eds.), *Exploring the speaking-writing relationships: Connections and contrasts* (pp. 134–141). Urbana, IL: National Council of Teachers of English.

Olson, D. R. (1981). Writing: The divorce of the author from the text. In B. M. Kroll & R. J. Vann (Eds.), *Exploring the speaking-writing relationships: Connections and contrasts* (pp. 99–110). Urbana, IL: National Council of Teachers of English.

O'Neill, M. (2002). *Nonprofit nation: A new look at the third America.* San Francisco: Jossey-Bass.

PRC (1995). *Mission Statement.* Springfield, MA: Author.

Pacanowsky, M. E., & O'Donnell-Trujillo, N. (1983). Organizational communication as cultural performance. *Communication Monographs, 50,* 126–147.

Paré, A. (1993). Discourse regulations and the production of knowledge. In R. Spilka (Ed.), *Writing in the workplace: New research perspectives* (pp. 111–123). Carbondale: Southern Illinois University Press.

Patnode, D. (1989). *Robert's rules of order: The modern edition*. New York: Berkeley Books.

Pearce, W. B., & Pearce, K.A. (2004). Taking a communication approach to dialogue. In R. Anderson, L. Baxter, & K. Cissna (Eds.), *Dialogue: Theorizing difference in communication* (pp. 39–56). Thousand Oaks, CA: Sage.

Percy Report (1957). Royal Commission on the Law Relating to Mental Illness and Mental Deficiency. London: HMSO.

Philipsen, G. (1975). Speaking "like a man" in Teamsterville: Culture patterns of role enactment in an urban neighborhood. *Quarterly Journal of Speech, 61*, 13–22.

Philipsen, G. (1976). Places for speaking in Teamsterville. *Quarterly Journal of Speech, 62*, 15–25.

Philipsen, G. (1986). Mayor Daley's council speech: A cultural analysis. *Quarterly Journal of Speech, 72*, 247–260.

Philipsen, G. (1987). The prospect for cultural communication. In L. Kincaid (Ed.), *Communication theory: Eastern and western perspectives* (pp. 245–254). New York: Academic Press.

Philipsen, G. (1989). Speech and the communal function in four cultures. *International and Intercultural Communication Annual, 13*, 79–92.

Philipsen, G. (1990/1991). Situated meaning, ethnography, and conversation analysis. *Research on Language and Social Interaction, 24*, 225–238.

Philipsen, G. (1992). *Speaking culturally: Explorations in social communication*. Albany: State University of New York Press.

Philipsen, G., & Coutu, L. M. (2005). The ethnography of speaking. In K. L. Fitch & R. E. Sanders (Eds.), *Handbook of language and social interaction* (pp. 355–380). Mahwah, NJ: Erlbaum.

Pomerantz, A. (1986). Extreme case formations: A way of legitimizing claims. *Human Studies, 9*, 219–229.

Pomerantz, A., & Mandelbaum, J. (2005). Conversation analytic approaches to the relevance and uses of relationship categories in interaction. In K. L. Fitch & R. E. Sanders (Eds.), *Handbook of language and social interaction* (pp. 149–171). Mahwah, NJ: Erlbaum.

Porter, M. E. (1979). How competitive forces shape strategy. *Harvard Business Review, 57*(2), 137–145.

Porter, M. E. (1980). *Competitive strategy: Techniques for industries and competitors*. NY: The Free Press.

Porter, M. E. (1987). From competitive advantage to competitive strategy. *Harvard Business Review, 65*(3), 43–60.

Porter, M. E. (1996). What is strategy? *Harvard Business Review, 74*(6), 61–78.

Powell, E. (1961). Water Tower Speech. National Association for Mental Health.

Prahalad, C. K., & Hamel, G. (1990). The core competencies of the corporation. *Harvard Business Review*, 79–91.

Psathas, G. (1999). Studying the organization in action: Membership categorization and interaction. *Human Studies, 22*, 139–162.

Rabinow, P. (1986). Representations are social facts: Modernity and post-modernity in anthropology. In J. Clifford, & G. E. Marcus (Eds.), *Writing culture: The Poetics and politics of ethnography* (pp. 234–261). Berkeley: University of California Press.

Rudd, G. (1995). The symbolic construction of organizational identities and community in a regional symphony. *Communication Studies, 46*(3–4), 201–221.

Rudd, G. (2000). The symphony: Organizational discourse and the symbolic tensions between artistic and business ideologies. *Journal of Applied Communication Research, 28*(2), 117–143.

Sacks, H. (1972). On the analyzability of stories by children. In J. J. Gumperz & D. Hymes (Eds.), *Directions in sociolinguistics: The ethnography of communication* (pp. 325–345). New York: Holt, Rinehart and Winston.

Sacks, H. (1989). Lecture six: The M.I.R. membership categorization device. *Human Studies, 12*(3–4), 271–281.

Sacks, H. (1995). *Lectures on conversation*. (Vol. 1–2). Oxford, UK: Blackwell.

Sacks, H., & Schegloff, E. (1979). Two preferences in the organization of reference to persons in conversation and their interaction. In G. Psathas (Ed.), *Everyday language: Studies in ethnomethodology* (pp. 15–22). New York: Irvington.

Sacks, H., Schegloff, E. A., & Jefferson, G. (1974). A simplest systematics for the organization of turn-taking for conversation. *Language, 50,* 696–735.

Salamon, L. M., Anheier H. K., List, R., Toepler, S., Sokolowski, S. W., & Associates (1999). *Global civil society: Dimensions of the nonprofit sector*. Baltimore, MD: The Johns Hopkins Center for Civil Society Studies.

Sanders, R. E. (1999). The impossibility of a culturally contexted conversation analysis: On simultaneous distinct types of pragmatic meaning. *Research on Language and Social Interaction, 32*(1&2), 129–140.

Schegloff, E. A. (1972a). Notes on a conversational practice: Formulating place. In D. Sudnow (Ed.), *Studies in social interaction* (pp. 75–119). New York: Free Press.

Schegloff, E. A. (1972b). Sequencing in conversational openings. In J. J. Gumperz & D. Hymes (Eds.), *Directions in sociolinguistics: The ethnography of communication* (pp. 346–380). New York: Holt, Rinehart and Winston.

Schegloff, E. A. (1995). Introduction. In H. Sacks *Lectures on conversation* (Vol. 1). Oxford, UK: Blackwell.

Schein, E. H. (1973). Can one change organizations, or only people in organizations? *Journal of Applied Behavioral Science, 9,* 780–785.

Schein, E. H. (1991). What is culture? In P. J. Frost, L. F. Moore, M. R. Louis, C. C. Lundberg, & J. Martin (Eds.), *Reframing organizational culture* (pp. 243–253). Newbury Park, CA: Sage.

Schwartzman, H. B. (1989). *The meeting: Gatherings in organizations and communities*. New York: Plenum.

Schwartzman, H. B., Kneifel, A. W., & Krause, M. S. (1978). Culture conflict in a community mental health center. *Journal of Social Issues, 34*(4), 93–110.

Scott, S. G., & Lane, V. R. (2000). A stakeholder approach to organizational identity. *Academy of Management. The Academy of Management Review, 25,* 43–62.

Scott, M. B., & Lyman, S. M. (1968). Accounts. *American Sociological Review, 33*(1), 46–62.

Sequeira, D. L. (1993). Personal address as negotiated meaning in an American church community. *Research on Language and Social Interaction, 26*(3), 259–285.

Sharrock, W. W. (1974). On owning knowledge. In R. Turner (Ed.), *Ethnomethodology* (pp. 45–53). Middlesex, UK: Penguin.

Shotter, J. (1985). Social accountability and self specification. In K. Gergen & K. Davis (Eds.), *The social construction of the person* (pp. 167–189). New York: Springer-Vedag.

Shotter. J. (1989). Social accountability and the social construction of 'you.' In J. Shotter & K. Gergen (Eds), *Texts of identity* (pp. 133–151). Newbury Park, CA: Sage.

Shotter, J. (1993). The manager as a practical author: Conversations for action. In *Conversational realities: Constructing Life Through Language*. Thousand Oaks, CA: Sage.

Sidnell, J. (2006). Conversation analytic approaches to culture. In K. Brown (Ed.), *Encyclopedia of language and linguistics*. Amsterdam: Elsevier.

Seibold, D. R., Meyers, R., & Sunwolf (1996). Communication and influence in group decision making. In R. Y. Hirokawa & M. S. Poole (Eds.), *Communication and group decision making* (2nd ed., pp. 242–268). Thousand Oaks, CA: Sage.

Smircich, L., & Calas, M. (1987). Organizational culture: A critical assessment. In F. Jablin, L. Putnam, K. Roberts, & L. Porter (Eds.), *Handbook of organizational communication* (pp. 228–263). Newbury Park, CA: Sage.

Smith, D. E. (2005). *Institutional ethnography: A sociology for people*. Walnut Creek, CA: AltaMira Press.

Spilka, R. (1993). Moving between oral and written discourse to fulfill rhetorical and social goals. In R. Spilka (Ed.), *Writing in the workplace: New research perspectives* (pp. 71–83). Carbondale: Southern Illinois University Press.

Spradley, J. (1979). *The ethnographic interview*. New York: Holt, Rinehart, and Winston.

Stokoe, E. H. (2004). Gender and discourse, gender and categorization: Current developments in language and gender research. *Qualitative Research in Psychology, 1,* 107–129.

Stokoe, E. H., & Smithson, J. (2001). Making gender relevant: Conversation analysis and gender categories in interaction. *Discourse & Society, 12*(2), 217–244.

Stokoe, E. H., & Smithson, J. (2002). Gender and sexuality in talk-in-interaction: Considering conversation analytic perspectives. In P. McIlvenny (Ed.), *Talking gender and sexuality* (pp. 79–110). Amsterdam/Philadelphia: John Benjamins Publishing Company.

Swales, J. (1998). Textography: Toward a contextualization of written academic discourse. *Research in Language and Social Interaction, 31*(1), 109–121.

Szasz, T. S. (1974). *The myth of mental illness: Foundations of a theory of personal conduct (rev. ed.)*. New York: Harper & Row.

Taylor, J. R. (2004). The search for sustainable organizational coorientation. In R. Anderson, L. A. Baxter, & K. N. Cissna (Eds.), *Dialogue: Theorizing difference in communication studies* (pp. 125–140). Thousand Oaks, CA: Sage.

Tichy, N. M. (1983). *Managing strategic change: Technical, political and cultural dynamics*. New York: Wiley.

Tompkins, P. K., & Cheney, G. (1985). Communication and unobtrusive control in contemporary organizations. In R. D. McPhee & P. K. Tompkins (Eds.), *Organizational communication: Traditional themes and new directions* (pp. 179–210). Beverly Hills, CA: Sage.

Tracy, K. (1998). Analyzing text: Framing the discussion. *Research on Language and Social Interaction,* 31, 1–28.

Trice, H., & Beyer, J. (1984). Studying organizational cultures through rites and ceremonials. *Academy of Management Review, 9*(4), 653–669.

Trice, H., & Beyer, J. (1993). *The cultures of work organizations*. Englewood Cliffs, NJ: Prentice Hall.
Turner, V. (1967). *The forest of symbols: Aspects of Ndembu ritual*. Ithaca, NY: Cornell University Press.
Turner, V. (1969). *The ritual process: Structure and anti-structure*. Ithaca, NY: Cornell University Press.
Turner, V. (1974). *Dramas, fields, and metaphors: Symbolic action in human society*. Ithaca, NY: Cornell University Press.
Watson, G., & Seiler, R. M. (Eds.). (1992). *Text in context: Contributions to ethnomethodology*. Newbury Park, CA: Sage.
Weick, K. E. (1979). *The social psychology of organizing*. New York: McGraw-Hill.
Weick, K. E. (1995). *Sensemaking in organizations*. Thousand Oaks, CA: Sage.
Weitzel, A., & Geist, P. (1998). Parlimentary procedure in a community group. *Communication Monographs, 3*, 244.
Weider, D. L. (1999). Ethnomethodology, conversation analysis, microanalysis, and the ethnography of speaking (EM-CA-MA-ES): Resonances and basic issues. *Research on Language and Social Interaction, 32* (1&2), 163–171.
Wieder, D. L., & Pratt, S. (1990). On being a recognizable Indian among Indians. In D. Carbaugh (Ed.), *Cultural communication and intercultural contact* (pp. 45–64). Hillsdale, NJ: Erlbaum.

Author Index

Adler, P., 15(n21), 83, *113*
Adler, P. A., 15(n21), 83, *113*
Albert, S., 1, *113*
Andrews, L., 80, *115*
Anheier H. K., xi, *120*
Antaki, C., 1(n3), *113*
Aristotle, 33(n46), *113*
Atkinson, J. M., 4, *113*

Bailey, B., 4, *113*
Bakan, J., xv, *113*
Baker, C., 55, 72, *113*
Barthes, R., 83, *113*
Basso, K. H., 26, 83, *113*
Baumann, G., 10, *113*
Berry, J. M., xi, *113*
Beyer, J., 33, 58(n74), 73(n88), *121*, *122*
Bittner, E., 73, 80, *115*
Boden, D., xiv, xv, 2, 21, 38(n56), 40, 74, 83, 84, *113*
Bridges, W., 57, *113*
Brown, P., 71(n87), 110, *113*
Burke, E. M., 33(n46), *113*
Buttny, R., 65, *113*, *114*

Calas, M., 9, *121*
Carbaugh, D., 2, 3, 3(n5), 10, 23, 25(n33), 26, 27, 29(n41), 38, 49(n65), *114*
Cheney, G., 1, 46, 53, 54, *114*, *121*
Cicourel, A. V., 84, *114*
Clifford, J., 11, 84, *114*
Conrad, C., 37(n54), *114*
Cook-Gumperz, J., 73, 74, *116*
Coutu, L. M., 93, *119*

Covarrubias, P., 4, *114*
Czarniawska, B., 71(n84), *114*

Deal, T. E., 9, 33, *114*
Deetz, S., 55, *114*
Drew, P., 6(n11), 34(n49), 94(n106), *113*
Drucker, P., xiii, xiv, 55, 58, *115*
Duca, D. J., xiii, xiv, *115*
Duranti, A., 34, 74(n89), *115*, *116*

Eckert, P., 6, 10, *115*
Eisenberg, E. M., 80, *115*
Elgin, P., 1, 2, 4, 4(n7), 5, 5(n10), 9, 10, 11(n18), *116*
Elsbach, K. D., 1, *115*
Emerson, R. M., 84, *115*

Felkins. P. K., 33(n46), *115*
Fitch, K., 11(n18), 26, 34, 94, *115*
Fitzgerald, R., 4, *117*
Fretz, R. I., 84, *115*
Frost, P. J., 9, *115*
Frumkin, P., xi, xiv, *115*

Garfinkel, H., 2(n4), 7(n12), 34(n50), 53(n71), 73, 80, 88(n103), 92(n105), *115*
Geertz, C., 2(n4), *115*
Geist, P., 37(n55), 38, *122*
Gibson, T. A., 25(n33), 26, 28(n41), *122*
Girton, G. D., 6, *115*
Glenn, P., 4, *115*
Goffman, E., 8(n14), 27(n40), 35(n52), *116*

Goodwin, C., 34, *116*
Gossett, L. M., 33(n46), *116*
Gumperz, J. J., 1(n3), 9, 9(n15), 73, 74, *116*

Hak, T., 83, *116*
Hall, B. J., 37, *116*
Hamel, G., 57, 60(n79), *119*
Hansen, A. D., 4(n7), *116*
Heritage, J., 4, 6(n11), 34(n49), 94(n106), *113*
Hester, S. P., 1, 2, 4, 4(n7), 5, 5(n10), 9, 10, 11(n18), *116*
Hogg, M. A., 1, *116*
Holtgraves, T. M., 4, *116*
Hoover, J. D., 49(n66), *116*
Hopper, R., 4, 34, *116*
Houle, C. O., xv, xv(n2), *117*
Housley, W., 4, *117*
Hymes, D., 2, 3, 9, 34, *116*, *117*

Irvine, J. T., 19(n26), *117*

Jablin, F. M., 13(n20), *117*
Janis, I. L., 45(n62), *117*
Jick, T., 57, *117*
Johnson, M., 27, *117*

Kanter, R. M., 57, *117*
Katriel, T., 34(n49), *117*
Kenefick, J., 21(n29), 62, *118*
Kennedy, A. A., 9, 33, *114*
Kitzinger, C., 4(n7), *117*
Kleinman, S., 83, *117*
Kneifel, A. W., 4, *120*
Knuf, J., 9, 33, 34(n48), *117*
Kotter, J., 57, *117*
Kövecses, Z., 21(n39), *117*
Kramer, R. M., 1, *115*
Krause, M. S., 4, *120*

Lakoff, G., 27, 27(n39), *117*
Lambert, A., 21(n29), 62, *118*
Lane, V. R., 1, *120*
LeBaron, C. D., 4, 34, *115*, *116*

Leeds-Hurwitz, W., 4(n6), 19(n26), 33, *117*
Lepper, G., 4, *118*
Levinson, S. C., 71(n87), 110, *113*
List, R., xi, *120*
Lundberg, C. C., 9, *115*
Lyman, S. M., 65, *120*

Mandelbaum, J., 4, 92, *115*, *119*
Marcus, G. E., 11, 84, *118*
Martin, J., 9, *115*
Meyers, R., 45(n62), *121*
Milburn, T., 18(n24), 21(n29), 25(n33), 26, 26)n36), 28(n41), 51(n69), 62, 79(n96), 82(n102), *114*, *118*
Mintzberg, H., 57, 58, *118*
Moerman, M., 10(n17), *118*
Moore, L. F., 9, *115*
Morris, M., 19(n26), 25(n42), *118*
Murphy, A., 80, *115*

National Mental Health Association, 33, *118*
NCCS Data Web, xii, *118*

O'Donnell-Trujillo, N., 9, *118*
O'Keefe, B. J., 74, 83, *118*
O'Neill, M., xi, xii, xiii, xiv, *119*
Olson, D. R., 79, 83, *118*

Pacanowsky, M. E., 9, *118*
Paré, A., 83, *119*
Patnode, D., 38, 50, 79(n95), *119*
Pearce, K. A., 35(n51), *119*
Pearce, W. B., 35(n51), *119*
Percy Report, 32, *119*
Philipsen, G., 93, *119*
Pomerantz, A., 4, 54, 92, *119*
Poole, M. S., 37(n54), *114*
Porter, M. E., 58, *119*
Powell, E., 32, *119*
Prahalad, C. K., 57, 60(n79), *119*
Pratt, S., 2, *120*
PRC, 12, *119*
Psathas, G., 6, *119*

Putnam, L. L., 12(n20), *117*

Rabinow, P., 84, *120*
Reis Louis, M., 9, *115*
Rudd, G., 4, 17, *120*

Sacks, H., 2, 4, 5, 5(n8–9), 7, 9(n15), 10, 17, 18, 19(n27), 22(n32), 24, 91, 91(n104), 93, *115*, *120*
Salamon, L. M., xi, *120*
Sanders, R. E., 11(n18), *120*
Schegloff, E., 9(n15), 22(n32), 26, 54, *120*
Schein, E. H., 9, 10, 57, 72, *120*
Schwartzman, H.B., 4, *120*
Scott, M. B., 65, *120*
Scott, S. G., 1, *120*
Seibold, D. R., 45(n62), *121*
Seiler, R. M., 92, *122*
Sequeira, D. L., 4, 19, *120*
Sharrock, W. W., 45, 83, *121*
Shaw, L. L., 84, *115*
Shotter, J., 27, 83, *121*
Sidnell, J., 9, *121*
Simpson, J., 55, *114*
Smircich, L., 9, *121*
Smith, D. E., 84, *121*
Smithson, J., 4, *121*

Sokolowski, S. W., xi, *120*
Spilka, R., 84, *121*
Spradley, J., 93, *121*
Stein, B., 57, *117*
Stokoe, E. H., 4, *121*
Sunwolf, 45(n62), *121*
Swales, J., 83, *121*
Szasz, T. S., 32, *121*

Taylor, J. R., 83, *121*
Terry, D. J., 1, *116*
Tichy, N. M., 57, *121*
Toepler, S., xi, *120*
Tompkins, P. K., 33(n46), 46, 53, 54, *121*
Tracy, K., 34, *121*
Trice, H., 33, 58(n74), 73(n88), *121*, *122*
Turner, V., 33(n47), 70(n83), *122*

Watson, G., 92, *122*
Weick, K. E., 40, 53, 53(n70), 92, *122*
Weider, D. L., 2, *122*
Weitzel, A., 37(n55), 38, *122*
Whetten, D. A., 1, *113*
White, K. M., 1, *116*
Whitticomb, S., 1(n3), *113*
Wilkins, R., 18(n24), 82(n102), *118*
Wolf Wilkins, K., 18(n24), 82(n102), *118*

Subject Index

Account(s, -able), xi, 6, 8, 11, 24, 28, 32, 58, 64–72, 73, 88, 89, 92, 93, 97, 98, 101
    Defined, 53–54
Action(s), vii, viii, 1, 6, 7, 8, 10, 11, 22, 23, 26, 27, 29, 31, 32, 34, 35, 40, 47, 48, 49, 50, 51, 53, 54, 58, 64, 69, 74. 86, 89, 90, 93, 99
    Culture in action, 10
    Symbolic action, 10
    Communicative actions, 11
Acts, 17, 71, 74, 75, 107
    Speech acts, 3, 31, 39, 54
    Communicative acts, 93
Address, vii, 11, 17, 19–20, 23, 24, 27, 86, 88, 92, 93, 105, 106
Agenda(s), 38, 41–43, 49, 59, 63, 73–75, 78, 79, 81, 90, 108 (n60, 108 (n62), 109 (n81), 110 (n89), 110 (n91), 110 (n92)
    Written agenda, 38, 41, 74
Anniversary, 25, 27, 29, 32, 33, 39, 40, 74, 100, 106 (n33), 107 (n43)
Annual Dinner (Dance), 12, 25, 29, 90, 91, 106 (n40)

Board of Directors, xiii, xv, 2, 12, 18, 26, 29, 30, 45, 49, 66, 67, 68, 69, 72, 82, 110 (n96), 111 (n96)
Board member(s), ix, xiv, xv, xvi, 1, 2, 12, 13, 15, 16, 17, 18, 19, 20, 21, 23, 37, 39, 40, 41, 42, 45, 46, 47, 49, 50, 51, 55, 58, 60, 61, 63, 65, 66, 68, 69, 70, 71, 72, 77, 79, 80, 81, 82, 88, 89, 90, 9, 105 (n26), 109 (n81), 111 (n96)
Boundary (-ies), xiv, 1, 3, 4, 7, 12, 24, 26, 27, 29, 34, 37, 54, 64, 86, 91, 93, 98
Business Communication, 87
By-Laws, 73, 79, 83, 87, 108 (n67), 110 (n96)

Category, 1, 4, 5, 6, 7, 8, 10, 17, 23, 33, 71, 103 (n8), 104 (n15), 104 (n17), 105 (n27)
    Category-bound activities, 55
    Social category, xv, 91
Center
    See Family Center
    See Puerto Rican Center
Collaboratively built sentences, 51
    Collaboratively Built Utterances, 90
Communication, 2, 3, 4, 10, 13, 15, 50, 57, 68
    Business Communication, 87
    Organizational communication, ix, 9, 13
    Communicative action, 90
    Communicative device, 58
    Communicative episodes, 93
    Communicative event, 54
    Communicative form, 50, 53
    Communicative practice, 3, 87, 94
Community (-ies), xii, xiv, 2, 3, 7, 10, 12, 20, 24–35, 37, 55, 63, 65–70, 85, 86, 87, 90, 91, 92, 93, 94, 95, 98, 100, 106 (n33), 106 (n37), 106 (n39),
    Community board, 30
    Community care, 32, 33
    Community center, 34
    Community context, 25, 27, 37, 86

Community (-ies) *(continued)*
  Community members, 30
  Community mental health, 32, 33, 93, 107 (n44)
  Community organizations, 30
  Ethnic community, 26, 107 (n46), 107 (n55)
  Interpretive community, 84
  Our community, 27, 27, 28, 30, 31, 32, 106 (n41)
  Puerto Rican Community, 26, 27
  Speech community, 2, 3, 4, 9, 10, 34, 91, 104 (n13)
Context, 8, 11, 13, 24, 25, 26, 29, 33, 34, 35, 37, 40, 65, 66, 83, 86, 90, 91, 92, 94, 95, 98, 104 (n18), 106 (n39), 107 (n49), 107 (n51)
  Business contexts, 70, 105 (n26)
  Cultural context, ix
  Institutional context, 111 (n106)
Conversation(s), 1, 2, 4, 5, 6, 7, 10, 11, 12, 15, 16, 23, 25, 38, 45, 50, 53, 55, 57, 58, 61, 62, 64, 65, 72, 73, 81, 87, 92, 93, 97, 101, 105 (n23), 108 (n62), 111 (n98)
  Conversational practice, 6
  Conversational resources, 34
  Conversational sequences, 11, 49
  Cultural conversations, 10
  Multiparty conversations, 24
  Organizational conversations, 10, 53, 64
Conversation Analysis (CA), 4, 5, 8, 34, 87, 92, 93, 104 (n11), 104 (n15), 104 (n17)
Coordinate (d), 1, 17, 39, 50, 56, 86
Co-President, 20, 22, 43, 45, 50, 59, 61, 62, 105 (n28), 107 (n57), 108 (n58), 108 (n62)
Culture, xii, xv, 3, 10, 16, 85, 87, 92, 93, 104 (n16), 104 (n20), 106 (n35), 110 (n88)
  Culture-in-action, 10
  Definition, 9–10
  Members' culture, 9
  Organizational culture, 9, 72, 91

Decision Making, 37, 39, 40, 41, 45, 48, 49, 50, 51, 53, 54, 86, 89, 104 (n20), 107 (n54)
  Decisional premise, 46
  Decision talk, 37, 54
Director, 15, 18, 21, 30, 38, 40, 41, 42, 43, 45, 46, 48, 49, 50, 51, 53, 59, 60, 61, 63, 67, 68, 69, 74, 78, 97, 110 (n96)
  Assistant Director, 15, 16
  Center Director, 66
  Director's Report, 74, 77, 78, 108 (n58), 108 (n62)
  Executive Director, 17, 18, 23, 26, 40, 71, 82, 105 (n25)
Discourse 34, 53, 58, 75, 106 (n35)
  Business discourse, 110 (n88)
  Discourse forms, 74
  Member discourse, 1, 2, 33
  Written discourse, 87
Documents, 32, 57, 73, 79, 80, 81, 83, 84, 87, 98
  Historical documents, 34
  Official documents, 76, 87, 90
  Organizational documents, 11
  Written documents, 13, 73, 74, 76, 100, 109 (n82), 110 (n88), 111 (n96)
Doubly Contextual, 34, 89

Elect (-ed, -tion), 12, 13, 15, 16, 17, 19, 20, 30, 65, 66, 67, 68, 69, 70, 71, 79, 105 (n23), 105 (n28), 108 (n61), 111 (n96)
Employee(s), xi, xii, xiv, 1, 2, 13, 53, 73, 85, 86, 109 (n72), 109 (n73)
Ethnic (-ity), xv, 1, 6, 16, 30, 35, 86, 88, 90, 92, 104 (n17)
  Ethnic community, 26
  Ethnic culture, 16
  Ethnic identity, xv
Ethnography of Communication (EC), ix, 2, 3, 4, 6, 7, 9, 10, 34, 54, 90, 92, 93

Ethnography of Speaking, 3, 8, 80, 93, 103 (n6)
Ethnomethodology (EM), ix, 2, 6, 7, 8, 9, 57, 87, 90, 92, 93, 103 (n4), 103 (n7), 104 (n13)

Facilitate (-ed, -or), 58, 59, 63, 64, 97, 105 (n29), 109 (n75), 109 (n76), 110 (n92)
Family Center (FC), xvi, 12, 15, 16, 17, 20, 21, 22, 23, 29, 30, 31, 32, 33, 38, 41, 46, 47, 50, 58, 59, 74, 75, 77, 79, 89, 93, 106 (n35), 107 (n44)
Field Notes, 11, 12, 80
Fundraising, 29, 39, 41, 49, 58, 59, 74, 78, 89, 106 (n35)

Gender, ix, 1, 4, 16, 19, 35, 88, 92, 103 (n7), 111 (n103)
Government, xi, xii, xiii, xiv, xv, xvi, 29, 30, 31, 32, 34, 91
Group(s), xi, xv, 3, 4, 5, 6, 7, 8, 10, 11, 12, 18, 19, 21, 23, 24, 27, 28, 34, 43, 45, 46, 47, 48, 49, 50, 53, 54, 55, 58, 59, 60, 61, 62, 63, 64, 67, 68, 69, 71, 72, 83, 84, 85, 86, 88, 91, 94, 98, 106 (n40, 107 (n55), 109 (n76), 111 (n104)
  Community group, xii
  Group identities, 4
  Group member(ship), 3, 7, 19, 23, 26, 54, 59, 62
  Groupthink, 108 (n62)
  Support Groups, xii, 13

Identity (-ies), ix, 1, 3, 10, 27, 37, 70, 79, 87, 93, 104 (n20), 105 (n26), 106 (n31), 106 (n40
Index (-icals), 8, 11, 34, 35, 58
Individual(s), 1, 2, 3, 7, 11, 16, 17, 19, 23, 24, 28, 29, 33, 35, 49, 53, 54, 55, 60, 69, 71, 72, 81, 83, 86, 88, 89, 92, 94, 97, 98, 100, 106 (n26), 106 (n40), 106 (n42), 107 (n46), 107 (n52), 110 (n92)
Inscribe (-ed, -ing), 11, 13, 73, 87, 92, 94

Interact (-ed, -tion), 1, 2, 3, 8, 9, 10, 11, 13, 15, 16, 17, 22, 34, 37, 40, 41, 45, 50, 55, 58, 60, 61, 70, 74, 76, 84, 87, 88, 89, 90, 91, 92, 99, 104 (n15), 106 (n40), 107 (n52), 111 (n106)
  Interactional moments, 29, 64
  Interactional sequence, 49
  Interactional structure, 73
  Social interaction, 5
  Talk-in-interaction 94
Introductions, 19, 20–24, 38, 63, 88, 106 (n32)

Label (s, -ed), xi, 3, 7, 8, 10, 11, 12, 17, 18, 20, 21, 23, 24, 25, 30, 33, 34, 50, 83, 86, 88, 91, 92
  Membership Labels, 11, 104 (n19)
Local Knowledge, 86
Long Term Planning, 62
  See Strategic Planning

Meaning (–ful), ix, xi, 3, 6, 8, 9, 11, 26, 29, 34, 35, 37, 40, 55, 72, 73, 74, 90, 91, 93, 111 (n106)
Meeting(s), 11, 12, 13, 15, 16, 17, 18, 20, 21, 24, 35, 37–55, 57, 70, 71, 72, 73, 74, 75, 76, 77, 78, 79, 80, 81, 82, 83, 86, 87, 88, 89, 90, 91, 97, 98, 99, 104 (n20), 106 (n31), 106 (n35), 107 (n54), 107 (n57), 108 (n58), 108 (n62), 109 (n72), 109 (n75), 109 (n80), 109 (n81), 110 (n93), 110 (n96), 111 (n98), 111 (n99)
  Board meeting(s) xv, 13, 15, 17, 18, 19, 20, 21, 25, 34, 35, 37, 39, 40, 41, 44, 49, 50, 51, 55, 59, 67, 69, 70, 74, 78, 81, 82, 88, 89, 91, 98, 105 (n26), 109 (n78), 109 (n81)
  Membership meeting, 17, 68
Membering Communication Analysis, 93
Member(ship) Categories, 1, 4, 5, 7, 9, 11, 13, 23, 24, 86, 92, 93
Membership Categorization Analysis (MCA), ix, 2, 4, 5, 6, 7, 8, 9, 10, 87,

Subject Index

Membership Categorization Analysis (MCA) *(continued)*
90, 92, 93, 103 (n7), 104 (n15), 104 (n13), 104 (n17)

Membership Categorization Device, 4, 5

Metaphor, 9, 15, 26, 27, 30, 57, 86, 106 (n39)

Methodology, 5, 8, 33, 91, 93

Minutes, 13, 15, 16, 38, 40, 41, 42, 43, 49, 51, 54, 66, 67, 68, 69, 70, 71, 73, 74, 75, 76, 77, 78, 79, 80, 81, 82, 83, 87, 90, 108 (n58), 109 (n81), 111 (n96), 111 (n99)

Mission (Statement), xiii, 39, 63, 73, 75, 76, 77, 97, 98, 100

Motion, 38, 51, 52, 53, 76, 81,

Norm(s, -ative), 3, 7, 8, 18, 23, 28, 37, 38, 54, 55, 57, 60, 64, 87, 88, 89, 101
Normal(-ize) 54, 55, 87, 88

Organizational Change, 57–72

Password(s), 93
Patterned Practice, 7, 35, 89
President, 16, 17, 19, 20, 22, 23, 25, 29, 30, 38, 49, 51, 58, 59, 63, 66, 68, 69, 71, 74, 77, 79, 86, 97, 103 (n2), 108 (n62), 109 (n86), 110 (n90)
Pronoun, 11, 18, 26, 47, 61, 90
Puerto Rican(s), ix, 1, 12, 16, 25, 26, 27, 63, 87, 88, 90, 105 (n22)
Puerto Rico, 16, 63, 105 (n26)
Puerto Rican Center (PRC), xv, 12, 15, 16, 17, 19, 23, 25, 26, 27, 29, 30, 39, 51, 58, 62, 63, 64, 67, 69, 74, 78, 79, 81, 83, 105 (n26), 106 (n33), 106 (n35), 107 (n43), 110 (n96)
Puerto Rican Time, 72, 106 (n36), 109 (n69)

Quorum, 51, 53, 65, 77, 87, 108 (n67), 109 (n80), 110 (n96)

Reference (-ing), 5, 11, 17, 20, 22, 23, 26, 28, 30, 31, 34, 41, 42, 58, 62, 65, 69, 74, 76, 81, 83, 86, 104 (n14), 106 (n32), 108 (n64)
Adequate reference, 5, 104 (n16)

Reflexively, 62, 93, 101

Relationship(s), xii, xiii, xiv, xv, 2, 3, 7, 8, 18, 19, 20, 23, 24, 25, 26, 27, 33, 65, 69, 70, 83, 84, 86, 87, 92, 94, 104 (n14), 106 (n39), 107 (n44)

Retreat, 20, 22, 39, 41, 58, 59, 60, 61, 62, 64, 78, 79, 106 (n31), 109 (n78)

Rite, 33, 109 (n74)

Ritual, 9, 24, 33, 34, 35, 37, 70, 87, 91, 94, 100, 107 (n47), 107 (n48), 107 (n52), 109 (n83)

Robert's Rules of Order, 38, 50, 83, 87

Role(s), xiv, 3, 13, 17, 18, 19, 20, 23, 24, 29, 32, 33, 41, 50, 59, 60, 62, 63, 64, 65, 70, 71, 73, 79, 81, 82, 83, 86, 88, 90, 92, 93, 94, 95, 97, 98, 100, 105 (n24), 105 (n26), 105 (n29), 108 (n58)

Rule(s), 4, 5, 6, 8, 9, 12, 18, 23, 38, 48, 53, 55, 72, 86, 87, 91, 107 (n55)
Consistency rule, 5

Secretary, 1, 11, 12, 13, 15, 16, 17, 19, 71, 73, 74, 79, 80, 81, 82, 86, 97, 99, 109 (n85), 110 (n95)

Sense making, 92

Sequence, 6, 11, 13, 20, 22, 24, 34, 37, 38, 41, 49, 55, 68, 76, 89, 92, 108 (n58)

Setting(s), xv, 3, 8, 12, 15, 20, 34, 59, 60, 92, 94, 95, 104 (n21), 107 (n46)

Situational Frame, 67

Social breech, 70

Speech acts, 3, 31, 39, 54

Speech community, 2, 3, 4, 9, 10, 34, 91, 104 (n13)

Staff, xi, xiv, xv, 2, 17, 18, 19, 23, 40, 45, 58, 78, 81, 82, 88, 105 (n25)

Strategic Planning, 58, 59, 62, 63, 64, 72, 73, 87, 110 (n92)
Structure, xi, xv, 2, 12, 21, 27, 33, 37, 50, 53, 57, 63, 73, 86, 87, 92, 94, 100, 103 (n2), 104 (n20), 106 (n40)
Terminate (-ion, -ing), 58, 64, 71, 87, 109 (n24), 111 (n96)
Treasurer, 41, 74, 79, 97

Volunteer(s, -ing, -ed), xi, xii, xiii, xiv, xv, xvi, 12, 13, 15, 22, 41, 46, 49, 54, 78, 94, 97, 105 (n23), 105 (n25)
Vote(s, -ing), 16, 17, 19, 23, 41, 44, 45, 50, 51, 53, 54, 55, 67, 68, 71, 75, 76, 79, 88, 108 (n62), 111 (n99)

Way(s) of speaking, 3, 10, 38, 49, 70, 90